Ecumenical Theology Today

ECUMENICAL THEOLOGY TODAY

Edited by

GREGORY BAUM, O.S.A.

(An Original Deus Book)

DEUS BOOK
PAULIST PRESS
(Paulist Fathers)
Glen Rock, N.J.

NIHIL OBSTAT: Gail Higgins, O.F.M. Cap.
Censor Librorum

IMPRIMATUR: ✠ Francis Cardinal Spellman
Archbishop of New York

July 3, 1964

Library of Congress
Catalog Card Number: 64-24514

COVER DESIGN: Claude Ponsot

Published by the Paulist Press
Editorial Office: 304 W. 58th St., N.Y., N.Y. 10019
Business Office: Glen Rock, New Jersey 07452

Manufactured in the
United States of America
24

Contents

5

Foreword

THE ECUMENIST, bi-monthly journal for promoting Christian unity published by the Paulist Press, New York, in collaboration with the Centre of Ecumenical Studies at St. Michael's College, Toronto, has been received, ever since its beginning in October 1962, with approval and appreciation by Christians interested in the ecumenical movement.

The success of the publication must have been due to the time of its appearance, the right moment, the year of the opening session of the Vatican Council. Though the movement for Chrisitan unity crystallized in the World Council of Churches has existed for two generations, it was only in the 'sixties that the great majority of Church leaders and students of theology as well as the general public became aware of the tremendous significance of the ecumenical movement. The reason for this awakening was, perhaps, the non-conformism of Pope John and his ecumenical policy. The startling change of attitude taking place in the Roman Catholic Church shocked Protestant Christians and made them more aware of the ecumenical endeavors of their own Churches. The general interest taken in the Third Assembly of the World Council of Churches at New Delhi, India, in 1961 and in the Faith

7

and Order Conference at Montreal, Canada, in 1963 were undoubtedly due to the awakening on the part of all Christians to the significance of ecumenism in the modern world.

In this general setting the modest contribution of *The Ecumenist* was widely appreciated. Not only did the number of subscriptions steadily grow but we also received countless requests for back numbers of the journal. Especially such articles as "On Mixed Marriages," "The Changing 'Y'," "Membership in the Church," "Ecumenism in Africa," "The Ecumenical Movement and the Jews" were in constant demand. Since our supply of back numbers is very low, the Paulist Press has decided to publish the more significant articles of *The Ecumenist* as a paperback.

Included in this volume are also three articles on ecumenical subjects written by the editor for other publications. We thank *The Thomist, At the Crossroads*, and the review published by the 32nd Couchiching Conference of the C.I.P.A., *Values in Conflict*, for their kind permission to reprint them here.

We have called this collection of articles *Ecumenical Theology Today* to remind all Christians in these days of easy association that the ecumenical movement must always remain a spiritual and theological movement. Our dialogue and our ventures of collaboration must constantly lead us to greater fidelity to the Gospel in our teaching, in our presentation of the truth, in our liturgical life, and in our way of holiness.

GREGORY BAUM
Editor, *The Ecumenist*

Part I

PROBLEMS
OF THE COUNCIL

1
Mixed Marriages and the Council

Gregory Baum

VARIOUS Protestant leaders in Europe and America have repeatedly expressed the hope that the Ecumenical Council will alter certain parts of canonical legislation on mixed marriages. What precisely do these Protestant representatives have in mind? Protestant Christians of deep conviction are just as opposed to mixed marriages as Catholics are. They believe, as we do, that the union between husband and wife should embrace the sacred as well as the secular. A married couple who cannot go to the communion table together are, in some real sense, divided. When Protestants, therefore, find fault with the Catholic legislation, they are by no means criticizing the strict attitude of the Church forbidding, in principle, the marriage between Catholics and Protestants.

Despite this general attitude, some men believe

that the ecumenical movement will weaken
Christian opposition to mixed marriages. In fact,
some pastors are cool toward ecumenism precisely because of this fear. Experience shows,
however, that the ecumenical movement makes
Christians more conscious of the positive content
of their faith and more attached to the sacramental life of their communion, so that the obstacles to a mixed marriage appear greater to the
ecumenically-minded. The naturalistic spirit, not
the ecumenical one, looks upon the union between man and woman in marriage as a purely
human relation and is indifferent to community
of prayer and sacrament.

Protestants, therefore, do not ask the Church
to encourage mixed marriages. They do, however, plead with Catholics to change certain
aspects of the actual legislation which they find
offensive. What are some of these aspects?

Aspects of Present Legislation

1. The terminology of certain canons of the
Code (C.I.C.) seems no longer in harmony with
the more charitable usage customary among
Christians today. Canon 1060, for instance,
speaks of non-Catholics as persons belonging to
"heretical or schismatic sects." Since the official
Roman documents of our century have avoided
the use of "heretical" and "schismatic" unless
these adjectives refer to persons in the act of
stubbornly resisting the Church, the C.I.C. could
be made to conform to this usage. In modern
languages, moreover, the word "sect" refers to a
particular kind of religious body characterized by
a peculiar outlook and mentality. It appears un-

just to refer indifferently to all separated Christian bodies as "sects."

In the same canon, 1060, the danger to the faith of the Catholic party which could arise from marriage with a non-Catholic is called "periculum perversionis." In modern languages this expression has an offensive ring suggesting moral corruption. A change here would be quite simple and charity seems to demand it.

2. The present C.I.C. does not distinguish clearly between an invalid marriage and concubinage, even though these two are quite different, not only in regard to legal consequences, but intrinsically as well. An invalid marriage, which is no marraige at all in the eyes of the Church, may be accompanied by the mutual intention to live in a permanent union, and hence differs radically from concubinage which is characterized by no such intention. According to present canon law, the children born of an invalid marriage are regarded as illegitimate, even though the partners, or at least one of them, may be in good faith. It is obvious, without giving any examples, that to many this law appears inadequate in the cultural situation of our time.

3. Canon 1102, § 2, forbids any sacred rites to be performed at mixed marriages. This legislation appears severe to Protestants. If the Church does permit a mixed marriage and the non-Catholic partner is a believing Christian, then it would seem that the Church would want to call the divine blessing on the couple, and stimulate in them the common faith in Christ and the desire for a holy union.

How could this be done? Many Catholic pas-

tors believe that some ceremonies should be permitted at mixed marriages. While solemn nuptial
Mass and blessing are proper to the wedding of
two members of the Church, simpler blessings
and the Mass of the day could be granted for
mixed marriages. Many Catholics feel that once
the Church has given the dispensation for a particular mixed marriage, the pastoral and liturgical action should be such as to induce a deep
Christian commitment.

4. Canon 1062 tells the Catholic partner in a
mixed marriage that he "tenetur conversionem
coniugis acatholici prudenter curandi." He is
obliged to work for the conversion of his spouse.
While a believing Protestant agrees that a Catholic will want to witness to his faith and, by word
and example, make his Church understood to his
family, the formulation of the canon does not
exclude methods of persuasion which invade the
freedom of the individual conscience and employ
questionable means such as threats, complaints,
constant lamentations, etc. Here again a new
formulation might be found. It could indicate
that the Catholic partner must not only give witness to the faith and desire to share it with the
non-Catholic partner, but he must also manifest
a real respect for the Christian conviction of his
partner and not despise his faith which he regards as his most precious link to Jesus Christ.

5. At present, the promises which the Church
demands of the non-Catholic party must be put
down in writing and signed. To many Protestants
this is objectionable. If they are believers, this
seems a violation of their conscience. Without
going into the various aspects of this vast prob-

lem and taking for granted, at the moment, that the Catholic Church must insist that the children of Catholics must be Catholic, the present legislation could be eased by putting the burden of the children's religious education on the Catholic parent. It would, then, be the Catholic party alone, who, after discussing the matter with the non-Catholic partner, would make the promises before the priest.

6. The points mentioned so far have been of secondary importance. They deal mainly with terminology and the range of application of the present legislation. There is one law of the Code, however, which is most offensive to Protestant Christians. Its change would affect the lives of many people and alter the ways of pastoral care.

Since the Council of Trent, the Church has demanded that all Catholics must observe the form of marriage laid down in canon law. Any Catholic who attempts marriage neglecting this form is not validly married. This legislation invalidates secret marriages among Catholics. But it also implies that a Catholic marrying a Protestant "outside the Church" does not enter into a valid marriage. His marriage is not only illegitimate; it is null and void in the eyes of the Church.

Valid Marriages

To Protestants this legislation appears very severe and almost arbitrary. The Catholic Church regards the marriage of two pagans or two Protestants as valid and permanent. Why then does she consider invalid a marriage of a Catholic and a Protestant performed "outside the Church"? A Protestant's confusion increases when he learns that the Church teaches the essence of the marriage union to be the mutual consent between the two parties. He does not easily see how an act of law could intrude into such a consent, rendering it incomplete.

Prior to the new C.I.C. of 1918 the Church, in certain parts of the German Empire, regarded as valid, though illegitimate, mixed marriages performed "outside the Church." Witness the decree *Provida Sapientique* of Jan., 1906 (Denz. 1993). Protestants desire that in countries where Catholics and Protestants live together and mingle freely, this decree would again come into force.

What is the Catholic attitude to this proposal? It is far from uniform. Many pastors are in favor of the strict legislation, believing that this is the most influential method of deterring Catholics from entering a marriage outside the Church. Other pastors believe that the more lenient legislation would, in the long run, be more beneficial to souls. They think that stigmatizing a mixed marriage performed "outside the Church" as illegitimate and imposing a censure on those who attempt it, should be sufficient penalty to deter Catholics from such unions.

What positive reasons do the advocates of the more lenient legislation offer?

(a) To protect the very idea of marriage. If a mutual consent to enter into permanent union can be invalidated by law, and if this law can be invoked after a couple has lived together for many years and produced children, then marraige itself might appear in the eyes of the people, as an institution created by human law. The strict legislation could ultimately weaken the Christian understanding of marriage and thus, indirectly, lead to many divorces.

(b) To facilitate reconciliation with the Church. The non-Catholic partner often refuses to have his marriage "fixed up" by the Church because the strict legislation obliges him to declare his marital union no marriage at all (even though he might have been faithful and self-sacrificing for many years) and to submit to a marriage ceremony designed for two people giving themselves in marriage. With the more lenient legislation, reconciliation with the Church would simply imply the absolution from the censure imposed by the Church.

(c) To protect the children and the marriage partner. The present legislation allows a Catholic to get out of a mixed marriage performed outside the Church, often with the approval of a priest and in the name of religion, although his motives are actually non-religious or even selfish (such as desiring to marry another person) and he is shirking his responsibility to his children and his partner in marriage.

2
The Problem
of Tradition Today

Georges Tavard

ON APRIL 8, 1546, the fourth session of the Council of Trent declared that the Gospel, which had been promised by God in the Old Testament and promulgated by Christ in the New, is "the source (*fontem*) of all saving truth and moral discipline," and that "this truth and discipline are contained in the written books and the unwritten traditions which, having been received from the mouth of Christ himself or from the Apostles under the dictation of the Holy Spirit, have reached us as though by manual transmission. . . ." (Denzinger: *Enchiridion Symbolorum*, n. 783). The broad meaning of this decree presents no difficulty. The Council clearly wanted to emphasize, against Protestant principles and practice, that the Catholic Church requires fidelity not only to Scripture, the written Word of God, but also to the apostolic traditions that have been preserved in the Church, insofar as these also convey the Word of God to us.

The question was to determine on what basis the Council would "confirm dogmas and restore morals" (*in confirmandis dogmatibus et instaurandis in Ecclesia moribus*—Denz. 784). Its first decree (session 3, February 4, 1546) had formulated a Symbol of the faith, which was identical with the Creed of Nicaea-Constantinople. Its second decree, at the 4th session, continued to lay the ground for the future tasks of the Conciliar Fathers, by establishing the Canon of the Bible and asserting the value of the apostolic deposit, both in its scriptural form and in its non-written form as preserved in the life, preaching and institutions of the Church.

A difficulty appeared, however, when scholars tried to deduce a theology of Scripture, Tradition and their interrelation from the statement of the Council of Trent. The statement had simply been a working principle for the specific purpose of defining the basis on which the Council was to work. It was not intended to be a résumé of a whole treatise on Scripture and Tradition. And though it was carefully drawn up and debated at length, it never had any other purpose than formulating the essential faith of the Church, without entering into theological controversies which already existed then among Catholics on the relative merits of the Scriptures and the Traditions. The doctrinal core of the Tridentine decree may be reduced to two points: the one "source" of all saving truth is the Gospel; the Gospel is present to us through the two witnesses of Scripture and the apostolic Traditions.

If we wish to build a theology of Tradition on the ground determined by the Council of Trent, we immediately run into two distinct problems, of which one is historical and the other speculative.

An Historical Problem

The historical problem concerns the exact meaning assigned by the Council to the word "and" *(et)* which, in its decree, unites the Scriptures and Traditions. Modern authors are not in agreement here. From the history of the Council it is well-known that the conjunction "and" in the final text replaces the expression "partly, partly" *(partim, partim)* used in the preparatory schema. For the late Heinrich Lennerz, this was merely a stylistic alteration: "and" would then mean "partly, partly," and would divide the Gospel into two distinct sections, the one contained in Scripture, the other in Tradition. "And" has then a *disjunctive* sense. Father Johannes Beumer interprets the change from *partim, partim* to *et* in the same way; but *partim, partim,* in his mind, means "on the one hand, on the other hand" rather than "partly, partly." It has an *alternate* sense. Professor Josef Geiselmann considers *et* to be *neutral.* According to him the Council was unwilling to pass judgment on the debated question whether Scripture contains only a part of the Gospel or the whole of it, and Tradition in its turn another part or the whole. (On these three positions, see Geiselmann: *Die heilige Schrift und die Tradition,* Freiburg, 1962; Yves Congar: *La Tradition et les Traditions,* Paris, 1960.) I have myself suggested that *et* has a *conjunctive* sense, inseparably joining Scripture and Tradition so that neither can be understood without the other (*Holy Writ or Holy Church*, N. Y., 1959).

This historical problem has been greatly confused by many theological manuals which, from the 19th century until recent years, have taught a doctrine that was a far cry from the statement of Trent: two "sources of Revelation," Scripture and Tradition, contain each a part of the deposit of faith. This departs from the Council of Trent on two scores. In the first place, Trent reserved the word "source" to the Gospel, and accordingly maintained its singularity; in the second, this source was not a source "of Revelation," since it was the Gospel, that is, the Revelation itself. The first Council of the Vatican was aware of this: in its Constitution *de Fide Catholica* (April 24, 1870) it repeated the Tridentine formulation, simply replacing the word *fons* and the expression *haec veritas et disciplina* by the phrase *haec supernaturalis revelatio*, thus identifying the one source of faith with Revelation itself (Denz. 1787).

The Counter-Reformation

Between Trent and the manuals, there stretches the militant theology of the Counter-Reformation, which stressed and overstressed the differences between Catholicism and Protestantism. It was not quite as one-sided as some have thought. Nonetheless, the Counter-Reformation effectively nursed the dualistic concept of the "sources" of faith. In the last decades of the 16th century, the notion of two partial sources of faith was well on its way to being attributed, against all historical evidence, to the Council of Trent. (On Canisius and Bellarmine, *see* Geiselmann, *op. cit.;* on Melchior Cano, *see* my "Tradition in Early Post-Tridentine Theology," *Theological Studies*, September 1962.) A good instance of this may be quoted from St. Francis de Sales who, unlike our manuals, respected the vocabulary of the Council, but read into it a distinction of contents between Scripture and Tradition which was not there: The Council

"expressly says that the evangelical doctrine does not only consist of the Scriptures, but also of the Traditions. Scripture therefore is Gospel, but not all the Gospel, for the Traditions are the other part: he who will teach other than the Apostles, may he be cursed; for the Apostles taught in writing and by Tradition, and all is Gospel. If you consider closely how the Council puts the Traditions near the Scriptures, you will see that it receives no Tradition contrary to Scripture; for it receives Tradition and Scripture with equal honor, because both are very sweet and pure brooks which have their starting-point in the same mouth of our Lord, as in a living fountain of wisdom, and therefore cannot be contrary, but have the same taste and quality and, joined to each other, joyfully water this tree of Christianity . . ." (*Les Controverses*, Part 2, ch. 2, art. I).

What the Counter-Reformation theology of two partial containers of Revelation really entailed still remains a moot question, in many cases. For it is hard to think that the theologians of that period knowingly contradicted the theology which had been universal until the decadence at the end of the Middle Ages, namely, the belief that all Christian doctrine is contained in the Scriptures as read and understood in the context of the Church's Tradition.

Cardinal Newman, for one, interpreted the Counter-Reformation benignly, in the light of the universal tradition rather than according to its expressions taken at their face value: "Nor am I aware," he wrote, "that later Post-Tridentine writers deny that the whole Catholic faith may be proved from Scripture, though they would certainly maintain that it is not to be found on the surface of it, nor in such sense that it may be gained from Scripture without the aid of Tradition." And Newman added: "This has been the doctrine of all ages of the Church, as is shown by the disinclination of her teachers to confine themselves to the mere literal interpretation of Scripture" (*Development of Christian Doctrine*, ch. 7, sect. 4, § 4-5).

Further studies are obviously needed before we may correctly appreciate the departure of the Counter-Reformation from the classical theology of the fullness of Scripture on the one hand, from the language and tone of the Tridentine decree of April 1546 on the other.

A Theological Problem

The historical problem that has been outlined should only serve as an introduction to a reflection on the nature of Tradition. Finding the exact meaning of the Council of Trent does not yet tell us what Tradition is. Our inquiry so far does no more than place the problem in its correct historical perspective. It will keep us from seeking the nature of Tradition in a side-by-side relationship to Scripture, as the theological manuals tend to do. Yet, besides providing us with this negative assistance, the history of the Council of Trent suggests a direction for a positive development on the nature of Tradition.

The Council's formulation begins with the identification of "the Gospel" as the source of all saving truth. Therefore in order to elucidate this, we need a theology of the Gospel. But unfortunately, we run afoul of two hurdles at this point.

In the first place, it is the Reformation, especially in its Lutheran form, that has developed a theology of the Gospel. This has placed Catholic theology on the defensive in this matter. Luther stressed the Gospel in opposition to the Law. This meant for him that the Gospel stands in judgment, not only over the work of the Law of the Old Testament, according to St. Paul's doctrine, but also over every ethic of Law that may appear in Christianity. Now the Counter-Reformation was precisely the period during which moral theology grew distinct from dogmatic theology on the one hand and from *lectio divina* on the other, thus acquiring the method and language that have made it, under the common denomination of theology, a separate discipline for which we have special chairs and experts. The Counter-Reformation therefore was unprepared to understand Luther's concern for an ethic of love based, not on the wish to keep the Law, although the Law will be kept as a result of it, but on the call of the Gospel, that is, on the initiative of the Spirit calling man in

Christ to salvation. (*See* Max Lackmann: *Der Christ und das Wort*, 1962.)

The Word of God

In the second place, since a theology of the Gospel is based on God's call, it requires a theology of the Word. Yet, since the Reformation, Catholic theology has frowned upon a theology of the Word that would be more than a theology of the Second Person of the Trinity. Still the Word of God is the Word, not only as spoken eternally in the Father, but also as spoken to man in time. "At sundry times and in diverse manners God spoke formerly to our fathers by the prophets, and in these last days he has spoken to us by his Son, whom he has appointed heir of all things, by whom also he has made the world, who, being the brightness of his glory and the image of his substance, upholds all things by his Mighty Word. . . ." (Heb. 1, 1).

God speaks to us in his Son. This divine voice is heard in the kerygma of the Apostles as perpetuated in the preaching of the good news by the Church. Thus this same Word is available to us in the Church herself and those who in the Church announce the Gospel are called to be instruments of the Word for the redemption of the world. The bishops, in the exercise of their apostolic teaching, and the priests, in their liturgical function and their care of souls, are ministers of the Word. The Christian people themselves, by the "royal priesthood" received at baptism, also communicate and express the Word.

This aspect of Catholic doctrine is now being

recovered and enhanced by biblical theology, by patristic studies and by a better knowledge of scholasticism, not in the sterility of what has become the static language of the manuals, but in the depths of its intentions and purposes. Yet we are only beginning to build a theology of the Word, which should be the heart of all pastoral concerns, of all piety and of all theological thinking.

It will be possible later, when this theology of the Word has become richer and more central, to elaborate a more profound theology of Scripture and Tradition. (*See* "The Holy Tradition," *Dialogue for Reunion*, Leonard Swidler, ed., New York, 1962.) Tradition is not, as it appears in the "manual" presentation, a static locus to which we turn for references, just as Scripture is not a static datum filled with arguments to prove doctrines and refute heresies. Scripture is the record of the manifestation of the Word and, by the same token, is a manifestation of the Word today.

Tradition is man's encounter with the Word in the Church. The two cannot be divorced, because Scripture is always read in the Church: this reading, by individual faithful, by bishops in Council, by the community at worship, forms the backbone of Tradition. Tradition is not super-added to another "source." For it is guided by the inspired expression of the earliest Tradition, which is also the model of all Tradition, Holy Scripture.

Such a theological development would start a chain of important pastoral reactions; for it would restore the scriptural depth to preaching as a proclamation of the Word. It would inspire important ecumenical initiatives; for it would enable Protestants and Catholics to meet on the ground of a common devotion to the Word.

3

Pacem in Terris and Unity

Gregory Baum

THE papal encyclical *Pacem in Terris* has been widely acclaimed as an instrument of peace in today's conflict-torn world. It is, moreover, a document with profound theological implications, some of them quite new and daring, on the Church's role in human society and creation. In this short essay we wish to determine the contributions the encyclical has made to the ecumenical movement. We will briefly consider three points.

1. Religious Liberty

Protestant leaders and spokesmen of other religions have repeatedly expressed their hope that the Second Vatican Council define the Church's position on religious liberty. They realize that two distinct views on this matter are taught by Catholic theologians in our century. Some theologians, the representatives of the older school, assert that error has no rights, and that therefore in "Catholic" countries governments should not tolerate Churches teaching erroneous doctrines. In such countries, they teach, the government should protect and advance the true religion. Only when Catholics are in a minority is religious liberty a good to be striven for, since in that situation it will favor the true Church. Other theologians, belonging to the newer school, the majority position today, teach that religious liberty is a good promised by the Gospel, to be announced and defended by the Church in whatever situation she finds herself. These theologians reject the idea that "error has no rights," since error is an abstraction and since people who err do have rights. These theologians derive their understanding of religious liberty from the notion of man and the notion of faith revealed in the Scriptures and taught by the Church. Man is created by God to seek him with his mind and heart and this requires freedom; and the very notion of faith, through which man is reconciled and united to his God, implies a free search and a free surrender. Man can be faithful to his destiny only if he follows his good conscience. From this understanding of the Gospel, these authors would say that interference and pressure by governments in the area of religion is never legitimate, except temporarily in unusual circumstances, when the exercise of a religion should interfere with the public welfare of society.

It is known that two distinct views on religious liberty have been proposed in the preparation for the Vatican Council. Many cardinals and bishops have indicated in public statements on which side of the controversy they stand, and there was a certain fear that the question would produce great conflict on the floor of the Council. Would it be safe to propose it to the Council at all? This is the background against which we must measure the papal declarations on religious liberty.

At the very beginning of *Pacem in Terris*, speaking of the rights of man which are inalienably his, Pope John declares: *Every human being has the right to honor God according to the dictates of an upright conscience, and therefore the right to worship God privately and publicly.* We cannot consider this sentence as simply addressed to atheistic countries, since then it would have sufficed to speak of man's right to honor God; the reference to the "upright conscience" suggests that the Pope refers to the conflicting theories on religious liberty. In another place he writes: *We must never confuse error and the person who errs, not even when there is question of error or inadequate knowledge of truth in the moral or religious field. The person who errs is always and above all a human being, and he retains in every case his dignity as a human person.* We must conclude, therefore, that the right to worship God privately and publicly remains in Christians who differ from us in faith.

Pope John, then, has taken sides in the controversy about religious liberty in the Catholic Church. This will have a profound influence on the discussion of this question at the Council.

2. Cooperation

Though cooperation of Catholics with other Christians and all men has been permitted and encouraged in the papal documents of this century, Pope John introduces a new sense of urgency for such cooperation and suggests that its area be greatly enlarged. He believes that at this moment in history as mankind discovers itself to be one, the common good of the human family emerges with such concreteness that it demands new forms of government, of authority and of cooperation among men. The Pope urges Catholics to take an active part in all aspects of public life and to work with all men of good will *for a progressively closer fellowship in the world of spiritual values.* Pope John does not simply refer to the temporal order as the field of collaboration; he makes it very clear that for him the concord of men on this earth is always something in which the grace of the Gospel is involved. He writes: *Human society, venerable brothers and beloved children, ought to be regarded above all as a spiritual reality.*

We must continually discover new areas of cooperation among Christians and among all men. The document *provides Catholics with a vast field in which they can meet and come to an understanding with Christians separated from this Apostolic See* and with other men of good will. In this context Pope John quotes a passage from his own *Mater et Magistra* recalling on the one hand that in such collaboration Catholics must take special care not to compromise, or be unfaithful to, the integrity of the Catholic faith, but on the other that *in their conduct they should weigh the opinions of others with fitting courtesy and not measure everything in the light of their own interests.*

3. Natural Law

Pope John's treatment of natural law is of considerable ecumenical interest. Though the subject deserves a detailed analysis, we shall briefly indicate in what area the ecumenical dialogue has progressed.

In many scholastic manuals, natural law is derived, philosophically or logically, from a concept of human nature as such. This approach has always been rejected by Protestant theologians and by many modern philosophers. Some thinkers object that a law derived from a conceptual definition of nature will not be able to correspond to the changes produced by historical developments in human society and in man. Some claim that a conceptualized essence cannot really express what man is; man is mysterious, they say, precious, of great dignity, but a riddle unto himself, and that it is by listening to what God has revealed that we discover who we really are. Others object to the neo-scholastic approach to natural law because, according to them, it is based on man's nature, *i.e.*, on what is common and general in man, and not on what is inimitable, and irreplaceably unique in him, namely his person.

It is with these opponents of the natural law that Pope John enters into dialogue in *Pacem in Terris*. He does not base what he calls natural law, on man's nature, but on his person! Though he occasionally uses the expression "human nature," he uses it rather descriptively as summing up what we discover about man through daily experience and reflection on history. Central in Pope John's thought is the person. It is the person of man, which we discover as unique and precious, to which correspond certain rights and duties as an expression of his dignity.

How do we learn what it means to be a person? The dignity of man as a person is one of the constants of human experience; and the progress of learning and the inventions of technology of our own age have brought to light new insights into the role that man is destined to play in this world. We have found in the past and have discovered in the present that it is a constant aspiration of man to be self-determining and responsible within creation.

The advance of science and the control of natural forces have elevated man to a new role of greater responsibility for the life and future well-being of mankind. A multitude of factors, which at one time were regarded as outside of human control, have moved into the sphere of human responsibility. The form of society, the Pope tells us, *must be adjusted to the era of the atom and of the conquest of space, an era in which the human family has already entered, wherein it has commenced its new advance toward limitless horizons.* There is a growing awareness of what man's destiny in the universe is. The Pope writes: *Men of our time have become increasingly conscious of their dignity as human persons.*

How is this insight, produced through man's reflective experience of history, related to divine revelation? This question is hardly touched in *Pacem in Terris*, since the Pope addresses himself to all men of good will on this earth. Yet, by citing some significant passages from the Scrip-

tures, the Pope shows that his understanding of
the human person and the possibility of human
concord are in harmony with the Word of God,
are supported and clarified by it. One may even
suspect that the moral discoveries made by man's
natural experience were possible because an added light from the Gospel made the ambiguity of
the world transparent. What is remarkable is
that the Pope does not seek "to prove" his understanding of the moral order and human dignity;
men of good will, he believes, will agree with him
on the constants of human morality. But if insight into the order of the world is conditioned
by good will, does this not mean that God takes
the initiative in the discovery of human wisdom
by touching the human heart?

The dignity of the human person is not the
only constant of morality. Another one is the
common good, on various levels, up to the universal common good corresponding to the whole
human family on this earth. Again we have here
an area of growing moral insight. These two constants, the dignity of the human person and the
common good of human society, are related to
one another in various ways, depending on the
evolution of society and the self-consciousness of
the individual, so that the actual formulation of
laws in society will undergo change and evolution. The principles of morality are absolute, but
the laws which govern society will depend on the
interrelation of many factors. The Pope writes:
*Social life in the modern world is so varied, com-
plex and dynamic that even a juridical structure
which has been prudently and thoughtfully established is always inadequate for the needs of society.*

Pope John understands the moral order of human society as based upon the human person and the interrelation of all men in peace and understanding, in harmony with the revealed insight of the destiny of man and creation, all conditioned by the good will in the heart—of which God alone is the author.

4

The Theology of
the Blessed Virgin Mary
at the Council

Gregory Baum

THE brief discussion on the role of the Blessed
Virgin Mary in the Church, which occupied
the bishops for a few days during the second
session of the Vatican Council received wide
publicity, publicity which was not always well-
informed. The discussion dealt with the question
of whether to treat the Catholic doctrine of Mary
in an independent document or whether to treat
it as part of the principal document of the Council, the schema *De Ecclesia* (On the Church).

The proposal that the teaching on Mary be
integrated into the schema on the Church was
emphatically made by a number of bishops who
regarded it as the task of the Council to show
that Catholic Marian teaching is part of the
Good News of salvation and that the special

graces accorded to the Blessed Virgin Mary belong to the *mirabilia Dei*, the wonderful works of God, promising redemption and reconciliation of mankind.

During the discussion, two diverse ways of understanding the role of the Blessed Virgin Mary in the Church emerged. Before the vote was taken on October 29, two cardinals were commissioned to present the two divergent viewpoints in speeches of considerable length. These two speeches have become significant documents, and since they were delivered on the floor of the Council hall, they have become public property.

Cardinal Santos' View

The first speech, made by Cardinal Santos of Manila (Philippines), defended the need and propriety of treating our Lady in a separate document. According to Cardinal Santos, the dignity and singular role of the Blessed Virgin Mary in the divine plan demand a separate treatment. Speaking of her only within the context of the Church might lead the faithful to think less of her than she deserves. While Mary belongs to the Church as a supereminent and altogether singular member, she is really associated with the bringing forth of this Church, both through her cooperation in the Incarnation of Jesus, *i.e.*, through her divine motherhood, and her compassion at the foot of Christ's cross, through which "she has merited with him redemption for us" *(pro nobis cum Ipso redemptionem merens)*.

According to Cardinal Santos, the Blessed Virgin Mary has a vocation to sanctity which is altogether singular, singular because she is the example of all others to be sanctified, and singular because she is the cause of growth in holiness in all (*auctrix sanctifications omnium*), both by meriting together with her Son the grace of redemption for all men (*gratiam redemptionis una cum Filio merens*) and by causing the application of graces to those who are to be sanctified (*applicationem gratiarum causans*).

For this reason the Blessed Virgin Mary is to be regarded as "in some way above the Church." Cardinal Santos cites St. Bernard according to whom Mary "stands between Christ and the Church." While Mary herself has been redeemed, her redemption differs not only in degree but in kind from that of other Christians, since she was preserved from sin and not simply liberated from it. Because, as mother of the Lord, the Head, she has cooperated in the production of his mystical body and because she was "by his grace associated with him in the objective redemption," her function in the Church is "essentially different" from that of other members in the Church.

According to the teaching of Cardinal Santos, the Blessed Virgin Mary is co-redemptrix of mankind and the mediatrix of all graces in the Church. He believes that while Mary remains always subordinate to, and dependent on, her divine Son, it is a truth to be taught by the Church that the human race has been redeemed by Jesus and Mary together. Many Catholics believe that this interpretation of the role of our Lady is not contained in the Christian Gospel revealed to the Church.

Cardinal Koenig's View

The second speech at this concilar occasion

was given by Cardinal Koenig of Vienna (Austria) defending the integration of Marian teaching into the schema on the Church. He gave theological, historical, pastoral and ecumenical reasons for his position.

Among the dogmatic reasons for speaking of Mary within the context of the Church, Cardinal Koenig referred to the need of overcoming the danger of treating mariology separately from the other branches of theology, that is, the danger of using one set of theological terms and notions in mariology and another set in the rest of theology. Through a methodological cleavage of this kind, the way is opened for exaggerations that are theologically unfounded and, in fact, false.

More positively Cardinal Koenig suggested that the Blessed Virgin Mary be treated within the document dealing with the people of God in its earthly form, in order to remind us constantly of the Church's eschatological destiny. Mary, in whom Christ has completely triumphed, reminds us that the people of God to whom we belong are still on pilgrimage, still on the way. At the same time by associating Mary more deeply with the mystery of the Church we will never overlook her earthly life in faith, poverty and humility. If we regard the Church, first of all, as an institution, Cardinal Koenig said, then the Blessed Virgin Mary, along with the whole company of the saints, is above the Church; but if we regard the Church principally as the people of God, and this is what the schema on the Church does, then our Lady belongs inseparably to the Church. In fact, by reflecting on the Blessed Virgin Mary in the context to which God has assigned her, we learn to appreciate more deeply the value and relevance of Marian teaching, and it is therefore in her honor that we desire to integrate her treatise into the schema on the Church.

The most profound theological argument proposed by Cardinal Koenig was the analysis of the Church's relationship to the unique mediator Jesus Christ, and the proposition that this relationship to Christ is analogous to our Lady's relationship to him. As the Church is the *fruit of the redemption* of Christ and, as such, is chosen by him as *means of salvation* for others (in which mediation each member of the Christian people has his proper and proportional part to play), so also was our Lady *fruit of the redemption* and, as such, appointed as *means of grace* in the history of salvation. And because Mary was the fruit of Christ's redemption in a unique and sublime way (she is, in fact, his holy mother), she also was an instrument of grace for humanity in a very special way.

Regarding our Lady thus as a type or figure of the Church, does not assign her a purely passive role in receiving the benefits of redemption. Just as the Church is not the fruit of Christ's work in a purely passive sense but is his instrument of redemption actively cooperating with him, so was the Blessed Virgin Mary, in the highest manner, actively cooperating with her Son in extending and perfecting the work of salvation. How did Mary exercise this cooperation? As the whole people of God are called upon to cooperate in the extension of the kingdom through the faith, hope, charity and prayer of each member, so our Lady, as the eminently holy member of this people, cooperated with her Son in faith, hope, charity, and intercession in such a perfect way that she summed up and signified the mission of the entire Church.

This interpretation of Mary's cooperation with her Son and the analogy to the Church's cooperation in the work of salvation, we may add, is actually contained in the Constitution on the Liturgy, promulgated by the Council on December 4, 1963: "In the Blessed Virgin Mary, who is joined by an inseparable bond to the saving work of her Son, the Church admires and exalts the most excellent fruit of the redemption and joyfully contemplates, as in a faultless image that which she herself desires and hopes to be" (§ 103).

Among the historical reasons for integrating Marian teaching into the schema on the Church, Cardinal Koenig referred to scriptural texts and ancient and modern ecclesiastical traditions warranting the parallel between the Blessed Virgin Mary and the Church. Among the pastoral reasons he quoted a South American cardinal expressing, in the name of many bishops, the hope that the Council will correct certain tendencies of Marian devotions in some countries that occupy the people with what is secondary and accidental, instead of leading them to the center which is the mystery of Christ. Among the ecumenical reasons Cardinal Koenig asserted the need to express Marian teaching in a way that the Orthodox Churches are able to recognize as their own teaching. He also mentioned that among

Protestant scholars the analogy of Mary-Israel-Church is being studied in the light of the Scriptures.

Cardinal Koenig concluded that by integrating the teaching on Mary into the schema *De Ecclesia* our understanding of both the Church and our Lady will become richer and more profound. It was noticed, moreover, that Cardinal Koenig emphasized the unique mediation of Jesus Christ, that he refused to assign to our Lady any part in the objective redemption wrought by the Lord and that he compared her active cooperation with Jesus to that cooperation which the whole people of God are called upon to offer to him. For Cardinal Koenig, then, our Lady cannot, in any theological way, be called co-redemptrix or universal mediatrix of graces.

We do not wish to outline here the brief controversy and the way in which it was resolved by making the Marian teaching a chapter in the document on the Church. *(See The Commonweal, November 22, 1963.)* The theological views proposed by Cardinal Santos are neither traditional nor universal in the Catholic Church. They are based on fairly recent developments and reflect a theology out of touch with the Scriptures and the liturgy of the Church. They can claim as support, however, a set of passages drawn from the encyclicals of several 20th-century popes.

Contemporary Studies in Mariology

The position explained by Cardinal Koenig is developed with erudition in contemporary Catholic theology. In recent years a number of studies have appeared, by authors of considerable authority, that have criticized very severely the mariological trends fostered in some theological circles. (*See* the vehement articles by Bishop P. Rusch of Innsbruck, *Zeitschr. f. Kath. Theol.*, 85 [1963]; also R. Laurentin, *La Question Mariale*, Paris, 1963; and A. Mueller's essay on mariology in *Fragen der Theologie Heute*, Einsiedeln, 1960.)

Of the greatest positive importance in contemporary mariology are the studies on our Lady's place in the Scriptures. A careful analysis of chapters 1 and 2 of Luke's Gospel has shown conclusively that the Evangelist regarded Mary as the daughter of Sion, the representative and, in fact, the holy representative of Israel, the faithful Virgin Jerusalem, who was visited by the Lord and brought forth the redeemer of the world. In Luke, Mary appears as the ark of the new covenant in which God has come to dwell in the midst of his people. Studies on John's Gospel and the Apocalypse have brought forward scriptural foundations for regarding the Blessed Virgin Mary as a type or figure of God's people, the old and the new people in continuity, guaranteeing the continuity between the two covenants.

It seems that from the beginning, in personifying the Church one has not hesitated to make use of the features of Mary, the mother of the Lord. (R. Laurentin, *Structure et Theologie de Luc* I-II, Paris, 1957; P. Gaechter, *Maria im Erdenleben*, Innsbruck, 1953; E. H. Schelkle, *Maria, Mutter des Herrn*, Leipzig, 1956; L. Deiss, *Marie, Fille de Sion*, Paris, 1959; J. Galot, *Marie dans L'Evangile*, Paris, 1958; A. Kassing, *Die Kirche und Maria, Ihr Verhältnis im 12, Kapitel der Apokalypse*, Düsseldorf, 1958.)

Patristic studies of the last decade have encouraged the understanding of Mary as a type or figure of the Church. The Fathers regarded the grace received by the Blessed Virgin Mary as signifying the grace which God bestows upon his Church, and conversely they understood our Lady as in some way reflecting in her life the role of the entire Church in the work of redemption. (*See* Hugo Rahner, *Our Lady and the Church*, New York, 1961; A Mueller, *Ecclesia-Maria*, Fribourg, 1951; Y. Congar, "Marie et l'Eglise dans la pensée partristique," *Rev. Sc. Phil. et Theol.*, 38 [1954] 7-9.)

Contemporary Theology and the Role of Mary

There is, moreover, the whole movement of contemporary theology which has profoundly influenced the mariological thought of our day. Several studies have elaborated in various ways the teaching that our Lady is a type of the Church. (*See* O. Semmelroth, *Mary, Archetype of the Church*, New York, 1963; Y. Congar, *Christ, Our Lady and the Church*, Westminster, Md., 1957; Karl Rahner, *Mary, Mother of the Lord*, New York, 1963; E. Schillebeeckx, *Marie, Mère de la Rédemption*, Paris, 1963.)

The influence of biblical and liturgical studies on Catholic theology has considerably transformed the context in which our Lady's role is understood. She is seen altogether within the history of salvation. Her place in this marvelous history is of greatest significance, since her role stretches from the age of the old Israel through the age of Jesus to that of the Church, and according to the doctrine of the Assumption she belongs, as the Fully-Redeemed One, already to the age of final restoration. From the wonderful things that God has done in Mary we can read off the destiny of the entire people redeemed by Christ, *i.e.*, the Church, the perpetual vis-á-vis of the Lord, his holy Spouse.

In particular the two doctrinal positions of Mary's co-redemption and her universal mediation, which have preoccupied mariologists during the first five decades of this century, have, thanks to the contemporary renewal of theology, largely lost their relevance. Prior to the biblical and liturgical renewal, the redemptive sacrifice of Jesus was regarded as concentrated in his passion and death on the cross and it then made sense to discuss the possible place of Mary in it. If, however, the redemptive sacrifice of Jesus includes his resurrection and exaltation, *i.e.*, if it embraces the whole paschal event, then the question of any other person sharing in its execution does not really make sense. Similarly, if the grace of God is regarded as gifts handed down from God to be received in the souls of the faithful, it is possible to speculate about the distribution of graces and the role of Mary in it. Contemporary theology, however, under the influence of scriptural and patristic studies, tends to regard grace not so much as gifts handed on, but, rather, as encounters with God in Christ and the effects of these encounters in us. In such a context the question of mediation in this sense through any other person than Jesus, true man and true God, does not really arise.

5

What Are Other Churches?

Gregory Baum

IN his opening address at the second session of
the Vatican Council Pope Paul addressed himself to the non-Roman Observers present in St.
Peter's as representatives of their respective
Christian communions. Several times in his
speech the Pope acknowledged the Christian
bodies separated from the Catholic Church as
"venerable communities," This raises the question, until now insufficiently studied by Catholic
theologians, of what these Christian communions
are. Are they Churches?

Churches in the Plural

Does it make sense to speak of Churches in the
plural? There is, after all, only one Church of
Christ, one Spouse of the Lord, and according to
the Catholic faith this is the visible communion
built upon Peter and the other Apostles. And yet

it is within the traditional Catholic vocabulary to speak of Churches in the plural. In fact, the Church universal regards herself as a family or body of local Churches united to the See of Rome and acknowledging its supreme authority. It is as Bishop of Rome that the Pope is the first of the bishops and holds authority in and over their Churches. It is to this family-character of the Catholic Church that Pope Paul referred in his inaugural address when he spoke of his election "to the episcopal See of Rome, and therefore to the supreme pontificate of the Universal Church."

A local Church is created in each place through the celebration of baptism and, more especially, of the eucharist by the bishop and his priests. In the eucharistic celebration (which includes the proclamation of the Word) by a successor of the Apostles, we have not only the renewal of the covenant and the communion of Jesus with those who are present, but with the whole covenanted people, the Church universal. Christ becomes present in the midst of his people offering with them and in them perfect worship to the eternal Father. In other words, the total mystery of the entire Church is present in the local Church. For this reason we may not regard the local Church simply as "a part" of the universal Church, as an administrative division, but rather as the presence or incarnation of the universal Church in one place.

Canonically speaking, one may refer to local Churches as parts of the universal Church; but in the light of theology one must acknowledge that through the bishop and his priests preaching

the Gospel and celebrating the liturgy, not only a
part of, but the whole of Christ's action as prophet, priest and king becomes effective in the
community and that, therefore, the whole and
undivided Church is present there. The Catholic
Church does not regard herself as a federation of
ecclesiastical provinces, but rather as a communion of local Churches with and under the Bishop
of Rome.

When we pose the question whether separated
Christian communities are "Churches," we do
not ask whether they resemble, or duplicate the
character of, the one Roman and Catholic
Church (this is, from the Catholic viewpoint,
simply impossible), but whether they resemble
sufficiently local Churches within the Catholic
Church to deserve, theologically speaking, the
name of "Church." In the strictest sense, and
this is well-known, we do not regard as Churches
those ecclesiastical communities which are not in
communion with the See of Rome. We believe
that by withdrawing from the communion with
Peter, a Church damages herself in her catholicity and enters into comparative isolation.

On the other hand, the official documents of
the Holy See have always referred to the Eastern
Churches separated from Rome as "Churches."
They have always been regarded as Christian
communions possessing so many elements making up a local Church, especially the apostolic
priesthood and the eucharist, that they were
acknowledged, in a real though limited sense, as
Churches. They are regarded as wounded
Churches. When the episcopal eucharist is celebrated by an Orthodox community, then, we

believe, with an imperfection that is difficult to define, the whole Catholic Church is present.

An Ecumenical Problem

This case is not really the thorny ecumenical problem. The Orthodox Churches of the East are well aware that we regard them as local Churches, even if we deny that they possess this ecclesial character in all fullness. The real problem which is constantly embarrassing us in the ecumenical dialogue is the Catholic evaluation of the Christian communities of the West, Anglican and Protestant. Since the Catholic Church does not acknowledge the continuity of the episcopally celebrated eucharist in these Christian bodies, she has never in any theological sense referred to them as local Churches.

In most of our studies on Christian unity and the relation of separated Christians to the Catholic Church, we have considered these Christians as baptized believers who have a real relationship to the Church of Christ. We have always taught, in varying terminologies, that through the baptism of faith a man becomes incorporated into the Church and that, therefore, Anglican and Protestant Christians are really our brothers in Christ, united to us in the same family, even if many obstacles keep on separating us. On this basis, ecumenical dialogue and Christian collaboration are possible. But the question remains: what do the communities of these Christian brothers mean to us?

The problem arises with a certain urgency in our contacts with the World Council of Churches. While this Council regards itself as a fellowship of Churches, it clearly and repeatedly asserts that its member Churches are not obliged to recognize other member Churches as Churches in the full and proper sense as long as they acknowledge in them a certain ecclesial reality. What "ecclesial reality" means usually remains undefined. In a practical sense this acknowledgment signifies that the conversations at the World Council are not conversations between individual Christians but between Christian communities. The member Churches of the Council regard one another not as purely profane or secular societies made up of individual Christians, but rather as Christian bodies, distinct from natural societies, with whom a dialogue about unity is possible.

Is the Catholic Church ready to acknowledge dissident Christian bodies in this way? Anyone who has taken part in ecumenical dialogues knows very well that in actual fact these conversations are always carried on between representatives of Churches. One never regards the Christian partner as an individual in whose personal theological convictions one is interested, but always as a representative of his Church. One takes for granted that the partner is an active and responsible member of his community, so that the fruits of the conversation will be shared by many and bring forth renewal in the Churches. For this reason, persons who live on the margin of their Churches are quite useless in the ecumenical movement.

This is the common experience in dialogue. But is there a theological foundation, and not only a sociological or phenomenological one, for regarding Anglican and Protestant communities as ecclesial realities?

The Papal Speech

Since Pope Paul's opening speech at the Council gives directives for further developments, it is worthwhile to give a brief analysis of his words. The section dealing with Christian unity is divided into two parts. The first one addressed to the bishops, tells them that one of the objects of the Council is the concern for other Christians.

By Christian baptism, the Pope says, these Christians have access to the perfect unity of Christ, but this unity is available to them only in the Catholic Church. And to convince the Council Fathers how real this inner tendency of baptism toward unity is, the Pope reports briefly on the development in the World Council of Churches. He refers specifically to the statement of New Delhi on "the unity we seek." He summarizes it in two points: (a) that there can only be one Church of Christ, and (b) that the hidden and visible unity which is meant to embrace all Christians must consist in unity of faith, the sharing in the same sacraments, and a mutually acknowledged and coordinated ministry.

What shall be the reaction of the Council, the Pope then asks, to these recent developments? The answer is clear, he proposes. We shall move toward greater openness, greater flexibility, greater acknowledgment of Christian gifts everywhere, in a single word, toward greater "ecumenicity" of the Catholic Church.

Pope Paul put this greater appreciation of other Christians into practice when he addressed, in the second half of the section on Christian unity, the Delegate-Observers present at the Council. He welcomed them as representatives of their respective communities, which he referred to not as "Churches" but as "venerable communities," and sent them fraternal and paternal greetings.

The Pope then entered into an unusual dialogue with them. He acknowledged, in words pronounced with great emotion, that if we have injured them in the past we now ask their forgiveness, and if they have done us harm we are willing to pardon them. He assured the Observers that the claim of the Catholic Church to be the One Church of the Lord is not an expression of pride or ambition, but rather a tenet of our Christian faith, and for that reason cannot disqualify us from the dialogue and fraternal peace. Perfect reconciliation is far away, hidden in God's providence, but what we are striving for now is this fraternal peace as a first step toward future reconciliation.

Seeing that the directives given by Pope Paul include the dialogue with dissident Christian communions and a real appreciation of the development in the World Council of Churches, the Catholic theologian feels impelled to strive for a deeper understanding of the supernatural character of these Christian bodies, especially since the Pope, in his speech, praised those Catholic theologians who have studied and exalted the authentic Christian patrimony in non-Roman Christianity.

Separated Communions

While, as we have mentioned, the dissident communions of the West do not possess the episcopal eucharist and hence do not allow an immediate analogy with local Churches within the Catholic Church, they must not be equated with profane or secular societies. They are religious bodies, and the specific principles that define them are Christian. The constitutive principles of these communities may be, in varying degrees, defective, but to the extent that they are authentically derived from the Gospel, Christian communities must be acknowledged as supernatural realities. They are not simply groups of individual Christians, but Christian communions in which means of grace are available to men and corporate worship is offered to God.

It is not easy to relate this positive evaluation of dissident Christian bodies to the self-understanding of the Catholic Church. The relationship of these dissident communions to the Church of Christ is unclear. Since the existence of separate Christian communions is against the will of God and mars the gift of Christ to his people, our divisions are a manifestation of the mystery of iniquity, and thus a factor of irrationality makes the relation of the dissident communions to the Catholic Church essentially obscure.

At the same time, we must be willing to acknowledge that these separated Christian communions proclaim the kingdom of God. They preach the Gospel, they celebrate holy baptism, and they declare the eucharistic signs in the midst of their congregations. There can be no doubt that they are instruments—in various degrees, defective instruments—through which God saves and sanctifies those whom he has chosen. And if God deigns to give grace through and in these communions and to accept the worship offered by them, then the Catholic people ought not to acknowledge this grudgingly, by way of concession, but with joy and gratitude, confident that this divine action, far from harming, will help the spiritual growth of the Church.

If a Catholic objected that most of his Protestant friends do not believe in the divinity of Christ or regard the Bible simply as a product of human genius, this would not necessarily imply that the Churches to which these Protestant friends belong have ceased to proclaim the Gospel, ceased to recite the Creed at their Sunday worship, ceased to baptize and to show forth the eucharistic signs in the community. We cannot judge a Church by the lack of faith of its members. We must evaluate it by the teaching it proclaims and the liturgy it celebrates. This is a principle that we demand also for the evaluation of the Catholic Church.

A Right Understanding of Ecumenism

It is important for us to reflect on the supernatural character of dissident Christian Churches since this will give us the right understanding of ecumenism. The ecumenical movement is not concerned with individuals; it does not consist in proclaiming the special self-awareness of the Church to other Christians to attract them to us. Ecumenism is not a subtle form of convert-making. A Christian who discovers the Catholic Church to be the place where the promises of God are being fulfilled, must follow his conscience and join her, but to persuade others of this is not the aim of ecumenism.

The ecumenical movement deals not with individuals, but with Churches. It is a movement for unity engaging the Catholic Church and the other Christian Churches in dialogue, seeking mutual understanding, finding wider areas of cooperation, and through discussion and research striving for greater balance in the possession of the Gospel. Ecumenism opens the Churches to the action of the Spirit drawing them into greater fidelity to Christ. In this way the Churches converge as they are being renewed. Ecumenism is not, in the first place, a matter of ecclesiastical negotiation. It is a movement of evangelical renewal, and as the Churches grow in the likeness of Christ they shall advance on the road to unity.

6

Communicatio
in Sacris

Gregory Baum

COMMUNICATIO IN SACRIS is a technical term referring to the participation of
Christians in the worship of Churches which are
not their own. *Communicatio in sacris* in the
strict sense signifies a participation in the sacramental life of other Churches, especially in the
eucharist, but *communicatio in sacris* in a wider
sense signifies a sharing in any form of prayer
offered by members of other Churches. The assistance of a Christian at the worship of another
Church is called *active* if he exercises a special
function in this worship as minister, godparent,
or someone in similar capacity or, in a wider
sense, if he shares in it as part of the worshiping
people.

Negativism of Canon Law

Present canon law forbids *communicatio in sac-*

ris. In canon 731, §2, it is forbidden to administer the sacraments to non-Catholic Christians, even when they ask for it. In canon 1258 it is declared illicit for Catholics to take any active part, or assist actively, in the sacred actions of non-Catholic Christians. The canon specifies that a purely passive assistance may be tolerated, for a grave reason, at non-Catholic funerals, weddings, and similar solemnities. Since Canon 1258 belongs to the section of the Code entitled "De Cultu Divino," the sacred actions in which Catholics are forbidden to share are undoubtedly the various forms of public worship of other religious bodies. Canon 1258 cannot be understood as prohibiting Catholics from praying with other Christians in a private capacity.

Since the directives of the Code are uniformly negative in regard to *communicatio in sacris* and do not make allowances for the difference between Orthodox liturgies and Protestant worship many commentators on canon law have thought that the participation of a Catholic in the liturgy of another Church is an intrinsically illicit action (Vermeersch/Creusen, *Epitome Juris Canonici*, ed. 1954, vol. III, p. 11). In the English-speaking world Catholic authors have even tended to regard as illicit any sharing in the prayer of non-Catholic Christians. This attitude arose during the history of Catholics in England. To attend the service at the parish church of the Establishment and to pray with members of that Church was, in the century of the Reformation, regarded as a sign of abandoning the Catholic position in favor of the Anglican Church. Even in their last moments the Catholic martyrs refused the consolation of common prayer with priests of the Established Church.

Some Deviations from Canon Law

The negative legislation of the Code however does not give a complete picture of Catholic practice in regard to *communicatio in sacris*. While canon 731 forbids giving the sacraments to other Christians, several decisions of the Roman Congregations have permitted giving the sacraments of penance and anointing to baptized non-Catholic Christians who are dying. Some canon lawyers extend these permissions to include the giving of the viaticum (cf. Vermeersch/ Creusen, *op. cit.*, p. 12). It is also legitimate for Catholics in danger of death, in the absence of their own priest, to ask for the sacraments from an ordained priest belonging to a separated Church. These practices show that *communicatio in sacris* may not be regarded as intrinsically illicit.

In regard to assistance at non-Catholic liturgies, forbidden in canon 1258, more positive practices have been received and permitted in the Church. Father Bevenot in his article on *Communicatio in sacris (Christian Unity: A Catholic View*, ed. J. C. Heenan, London, 1962) shows that in some areas in the East ecclesiastical customs have existed for centuries according to which the mutual liturgical participation of Catholics and Orthodox was, under certain circumstances, a licit thing, even in such sacred actions as preaching and the hearing of confessions. It was only toward the end of the 18th

century that a stricter legislation prohibited
these practices. Even today in certain parts of
the Near East liturgical customs regarding *communicatio in sacris* often go beyond the letter of
canon law. In some villages and towns Catholics
attend Orthodox eucharistic liturgies when no
Catholic priest is available, and at Catholic
schools Orthodox children are permitted to receive holy communion when they have no access
to their own worship.

At the Vatican Council many Fathers, especially among the Eastern bishops, insisted that
the legislation regarding *communicatio in sacris*
be mitigated. According to the *Herder Correspondence* (I, March 1964, 77) some Eastern
Fathers called for a restoration of the practice
before 1949 according to which it was possible,
under certain circumstances, to receive the
eucharist in a Church not one's own.

Since it is clear from the practice of the
Church that *communicatio in sacris* is not intrinsically illicit, we must find the theological
principles which determine whether it should be
forbidden or allowed. It is obvious that the application of these principles will differ according to
whether they are applied to Catholic-Orthodox
or Catholic-Protestant relations. The Church's
attitude to the sacramental liturgy of the Orthodox, founded on the consecration of bishops and
reflecting the unabridged faith of the ancient
Church, differs considerably from her attitude to
the worship of a Church where she is unable to
acknowledge valid episcopal consecration or the
sacramental celebration of the eucharist. Are
there principles which are general enough to be

applied to all situations in which the Catholic Church finds herself?

Reasons for Prohibition

Let us consider first the reasons why, as a general rule, *communicatio in sacris* has been prohibited by law.

(1) Since the official worship of any Church is the deepest expression of her faith and teaches the whole of her doctrine, no one can take part in such a worship unless he accepts the teaching of this Church.

(2) Since the liturgy, especially the holy eucharist, is the sign of the Church's unity assembling its members at the banquet of the Lord, the participation of a non-member in these rites would make the sign of unity deceptive. To say that Christians are divided means precisely that they are unable to eat at the same holy table; and to say that Christians seek reconciliation in a single Church, the aim of the ecumenical movement, means that then, and only then, will they be able to celebrate the eucharist at the same table.

(3) The third argument against *communicatio in sacris*, which applies not only to participation in official liturgies but to all forms of prayer with others, is the danger of indifferentism and confusion in the Christian community. There were times in the past when taking part in the worship of others, even at private prayer ceremonies in a family might have been regarded as a grave act of disloyalty to the Catholic Church. In the more recent past the sharing of public or private prayers may have misled the Christian people, both

Catholic and Protestant, into believing that the Catholic Church regarded herself as one Church among others of equal authenticity. Such a sharing might have inspired an indifference to revealed truth or created the illusion that the unity of Christians had already been achieved. However, thanks to the ecumenical movement and the education it has produced among the people, there are today many areas and many situations where the participation in the worship of others does not create these dangers.

These various reasons against the *communicatio in sacris* arise from the understanding of liturgy as *sign of unity*, that is, as manifesting the unity of faith, the unity of new life, and the unity of the social body.

Liturgy as Means of Grace

Yet this is not the only aspect under which one may regard the liturgy of the Church. Liturgy is also a *means of grace*. It is the instrument chosen by God to sanctify men and to transform human society. This is the principle on which are based the permissions for Catholic priests to give the sacraments to dying non-Catholic Christians and for Catholics in danger of death to receive the sacraments from non-Catholic priests. In these cases *communicatio in sacris* is a necessary means of grace for people at a moment when the role of liturgy to signify unity does not have to be considered.

The liturgy considered as means of grace is the principle enabling the ecclesiastical legislator to permit *communicatio in sacris* whenever the need of salvation and sanctification make it reasonable, as long as the dangers arising from the momentary neglect of the liturgy as sign of unity are negligible. One may imagine that the Council Fathers of the East who have asked for a more generous legislation in regard to *communicatio in sacris*, even in the eucharistic celebration, had in mind a wide application of this principle whenever Catholic or Orthodox Christians living away from their parishes would be unable to receive the sacraments without this permission.

The liturgy is not only a means of grace for individuals; it is also a means chosen by God to affect the Christian community. To participate in the worship of another Church could be a means of furthering charity among Christians or of manifesting the unity of grace and baptism which already exists among separated brothers. This kind of sharing would accelerate the quest for Christian unity. At times this kind of limited *communicatio in sacris* may be a means of creating greater love in a family or some other human society. In such cases the ecclesiastical legislator could permit *communicatio in sacris* as long as the momentary neglect of the liturgy as sign of unity would not confuse the Christian conscience or, in particular, create the danger of indifferentism. This positive principle is, in fact, applied whenever Catholics are permitted to take part in Protestant or inter-denominational worship services at ecumenical gatherings, at civic functions and on other occasions. While the question of eucharistic communion between Catholics and Protestants has not seriously arisen for the simple reason that we differ in our doctrine on what Jesus does to us in the eucharistic mystery, the question of common prayer in liturgical services arises all the time. In particular the problem of an occasional assistance at a Protestant worship for valid personal reasons arises very frequently. In these situations where the *communicatio in sacris*, while not supplying a necessary means of grace, nevertheless represents a suitable means of fostering Christian unity or personal charity, the ecclesiastical legislator could grant permission or personal conscience could counsel it as long as the dangers arising from the neglect of the sign of unity implicit in worship are, as a result of the ecumenical movement, regarded as negligible.

Two Principles

If our analysis is correct, then we may say that *communicatio in sacris* is ruled by two principles, one of which forbids it while the other favors it. Regarding the sacred actions or worship as a sign of unity, *communicatio in sacris* becomes impossible, but regarding it as a means of grace, *communicatio in sacris* may be permitted. We have here a case which often arises in theological reflection on ecclesiastical practices: we find that the practice is governed by two principles which tend in opposite directions. In such cases it is normally up to the ecclesiastical legislator, *i.e.* either to the common law of the Church or to episcopal authority, to judge which of the two principles is to be regarded as having more weight in a particular situation. In our case this would mean that, after the introduction of a more positive canon law, the episcopal authority in a certain area could decide on what occasions the principle prohibiting, or on what occasions the principle permitting, *communicatio in sacris* predominated.

Such a renewed legislation would enable the bishops of the Christian East to allow *communicatio in sacris* in places and on occasions where they judge it to be important. At the same time it would give the bishops of the West, where the problem poses itself in different circumstances, the principles by which they could make decisions in their own dioceses. They would be able to permit a limited *communicatio in sacris* on certain occasions where common worship would be a means of fostering the ecumenical movement, if they judged that their people and public opinion were sufficiently well-instructed not to be misled into indifferentism.

Part II

THE
CATHOLIC CHURCH

7

Who Belongs
to the Church?

Gregory Baum

THE question of Church membership is difficult
because, according to Catholic belief, the
Church is at one and the same time an institution
containing the means of grace (Gospel and sacraments) and a fellowship of men in union with
Christ. The Church is both of these essentially,
even if she is an institution only as a means to an
end, which is this fellowship. If we put the main
emphasis on the institutional character of the
Church, we tend to define membership in institutional or canonical terms, and if we put the main
stress on the new life which this institution produces in humanity, we come to a wider notion of
membership in terms of redemption and brotherhood.

It is not surprising, therefore, that there is a
controversy in Catholic theology between two

different views on membership in the Church. One of the points of this essay is to show that the difference between these two views is, today, largely one of terminology.

The Notion of Univocal Membership

One school of theologians looks upon the Church principally as a visible institution and hence regards the notion of membership as univocal, meaning that it does not admit of degrees. This school believes that one is either a member of the Church or one is not: membership can never be a question of more or less. To be a member of the Church in any real sense one must, according to these theologians, bear the triple mark of baptism, Catholic creed, and ecclesiastical communion, which means that only Roman Catholics are members of the Mystical Body.

The *contemporary* proponents of this view do not doubt that there are Christians outside the visible boundaries of the Church. They do not doubt that the Christian message preached outside the Church and the sacraments received beyond the borders of the Catholic community are able to produce new life and communicate the Holy Spirit to those who cling to the message and the sacraments in faith. They assert quite strongly that there exists some community of grace and fellowship among all believers reborn in baptism and that in some way the Holy Spirit is shared by all true Christians. But what they deny is that these Christians outside the visible boundaries of the Church, even when they are as close to us as the Orthodox and alive with true Christian holiness, are in any proper sense members of the Church of the Lord. They may have a real relationship to the Church, they may be said to adhere to it from the outside, but, however abundant the gifts of grace, they are not members.

The theologians holding that membership is a univocal notion usually quote from Pope Pius XII's encyclical *Mystici Corporis,* in which he writes: "Only those are to be accounted real and actual members of the Church who have been regenerated in the waters of baptism, who profess the true faith, and who have not detached themselves from the structure of the Body unto their own undoing or have been cut off for a great crime by legitimate authority." Pius XII, however, did not intend to solve the theological controversy, since, by denying membership to those who "have detached themselves from the Body unto their own undoing" he left the question open in regard to those who have never willfully detached themselves from the visible structure of the Church but were born and reborn outside of it.

The Notion of Degrees of Membership

There exists, therefore, another school of theologians who regard the notion of membership in the Church as analogous, admitting of degrees. They also believe that the Catholic Church is the unique manifestation of Christ's Mystical Body on earth, but they deny that dissident Christians united to their Lord through baptism and the message of faith may be regarded as outside the Church. The bond uniting them to the Church is visible, since creed and sacrament have fashioned it. Roman Catholics possess canonically speaking, *perfect* membership in the Church; at the same time believing dissident Christians, reborn in baptism, are in a real and actual sense members of the Mystical Body, even if their membership is institutionally *imperfect, i.e.* even if they do not have access to all the gifts Christ has bestowed upon his Church.

One of the principal arguments for this position is the biblical and traditional doctrine of Christian baptism, summarized by Leo XIII in a sentence in his encyclical *Annum Sacrum* and cited a generation later by Pius XI in his encyclical *Quas Primas*: "Those who have been validly cleansed by the waters of baptism belong by right to the Church, even if error keep them apart or disagreement sever them from the community." (*See* Baum, *That They May Be One*, Newman Press, Westminster, Md., p. 39).

It is well-known from his lectures and articles that this is the position of Cardinal Bea, the president of the Secretariat for Promoting Christian Unity. Here is a typical sentence of his: "The Catholic Church categorically affirms that, according to the general doctrine of the New Testament, through valid baptism, even when received outside the Roman Church, the baptized person is organically united to Christ and his Mystical Body" (*Documentation Catholique*, 60 [Jan. 6, 1963] col. 82; *see* also Card. Bea, *Position of Catholics regarding Church Unity*, Paulist Press, 1961).

The particular theological advantage of this position over the first is that it clearly distinguishes the salvational situation of Orthodox and

Protestant Christians from the situation of men who do not have the Christian faith though, being touched by God's grace and having submitted to the divine will in their hearts, they are also attached to the body of salvation in the world. By denying membership in the Church to dissident baptized Christians, one seems to place them in the rather vague category of men of good will and belittle the sacramental links and the real fellowship between them and ourselves.

There can be little doubt that the main trend of modern ecclesiology is in favor of the second position. (*See* S. Jaki, *Les tendances nouvelles de l'ecclésiologie*, Rome, 1957, p. 241.) The more profound our theological approach to the Church and the more ready we are to regard her as the universal means of redemption in the world, the more necessary it becomes to acknowledge several ways of belonging to her, *i.e.* to consider membership as an analogous concept. To assert the universal mediation of the Catholic Church and to regard membership as a univocal notion, *i.e.* to reject membership in various degrees, would ultimately lead to a sectarian position.

At the moment, however, it seems to me that the difference between the two positions is principally one of terminology. Both schools admit that the Church of Rome is the unique community of the Lord joined to him as his earthly body, and both acknowledge that Christians outside the visible boundaries of the Church have access to the life of grace which Christ communicates through his message and sacraments. All Catholic theologians of our day agree, therefore, in the evaluation of the objective situation of dissident Christians.

A Decision for Second Vatican Council?

Will the Second Vatican Council resolve this controversy? From the public statements of bishops and cardinals we know that many of them desire this, some on one side and some on the other. There is, however, a third position which asserts that it would be better if the Council left open the question of membership in the Church. Since we have a canonical definition of who belongs to the Church and hence are able to solve the practical problems of pastoral life, there is no urgency to solve the question on the deeper level of theology. One might even go further and say: The Church that claims to be universal should refuse to define its own boundaries in the world.

What are the reasons for this position? The Church was created by what Christ did for us on the cross, and since the people purchased by Christ on the cross was the whole human family, there exists a basic identification between the Church and the humanity into which she is sent. This identification is acknowledged constantly by the Church in her faith and her prayer. Because of the intentional unity between the Church and humanity, the grace of Christ is active everywhere in the world. Even though the means of grace are concentrated in a singular and complete fashion in the visible Church, all of humanity has been touched by the redemptive work of the Lord and his saving grace appeals to the hearts of men everywhere, preparing and initiating the kingdom. As in the Israel of old there was "Church before the Church," so now in the world there is "Church outside the Church." Since the community of the Lord calls her own that part of humanity which has been touched and renewed, however partially, by the redemption of Christ, she will refuse to define her own limits. She will never say: "I only stretch to this line, and you, beyond, don't belong to me any more."

Especially in our own day it is of great importance that in announcing the Christian message we do not only declare the separation of the Church from the world of the unredeemed, but that with equal confidence we proclaim the Church to be the sacrament of humanity, the divine instrument of a transforming movement that is universal.

The Church has not been sent to divide but to unite. Men are sometimes tempted to regard the Church as a divisive force in the world, separating Christians from non-Christians and Catholics from non-Catholics, while actually the only true dividing factor in the human race is the personal choice between holiness and evil, and this decision maps out a line which does not coincide with the canonical borders of the Church. The fundamental opposition in the world is not between the Church and others, but between those who, by God's grace, are of good will and those who have hardened their hearts in malice; and when we speak of the Church as the sacrament of humanity we confidently assert that God mediates this good will, wherever it may be found, through her. Since the canonical limits of the Church are well established in Catholic teaching, the Council may consider it as an urgent task to announce the Church's mission to unify mankind and to spell out the real relation existing between her and all men.

There is a second reason, one which directly pertains to ecumenism, why some wish that the Council does not define who is a member of the Church. Since dissident Christians are linked to us in many visible ways and therefore most certainly belong to the family of God, is it really fortunate to refer to them as "imperfect" or "incomplete" members of the Church? Will Orthodox and Protestant Christians be glad when they are told that they are basically Roman Catholics without realizing it? They will not: they will feel that we do not fully appreciate the role and dignity of their own ecclesiastical communions before God.

What are dissident Christian communions to us? According to Catholic doctrine, they are *not* branches or organs of the Church universal and hence cannot strictly be called local Churches. But what can we say about these communions in a positive way? They certainly contain many means of grace of the Church, in varying degrees, elements through which they communicate to their faithful a share in the life of Christ and the guidance of the Spirit. Because dissident communions mediate the Christian life, despite the principles of division contained in them, several modern Catholic theologians are willing to call them Churches, or local Churches, in an *analogous* way, and this analogy is here not simply extrinsic, of designation, but intrinsic and ontological.

These questions have not yet matured in the minds of Catholic teachers. It may well be argued that one should refrain from telling dissident Christians that they are members of the Church, until the time when one could also tell them what their communions mean to us in terms of the Gospel.

The difference between the three positions outlined in this article is not so much a matter of doctrine as of emphasis.

8
Papacy
and Episcopacy

Gregory Baum

THE First Vatican Council defined the primacy
of the Roman pontiff. We profess, therefore,
that the bishop of Rome is an infallible teacher of
the Gospel and that he holds universal jurisdiction over the whole Church. The First Vatican
Council specified that this jurisdiction is immediate and ordinary, in other words truly episcopal, and hence we are justified in calling the pope
the universal bishop of the Church.

At the same time the pope is not the only
bishop. In fact, bishops are as essential to the
Catholic Church as he is. Despite his primacy, he
could never dispense with the episcopal structure
of the Church universal and administer the Catholic people through a system of government more
directly under his control. The First Vatican itself made this clear.

This, however, was all that the First Vatican

said about bishops in the Church. The original
document prepared for the conciliar deliberations
included fifteen chapters on the Church and her
constitution, but the briefness of the session did
not permit the bishops to discuss more than the
chapter dealing with papal primacy. Since the
Council did not deal with the role of bishops in
the Church nor define their relationship to the
Roman pontiff, the impression was created in
many quarters outside the Church that the
Council had suppressed the episcopal structure
of the Catholic Church and introduced a papal
government in its stead. The accusations became
vocal in terms such as "episcopal jurisdiction has
been absorbed into papal," "the pope no longer
exercises certain reserved rights, as he has in the
past, but now holds the whole of the bishops'
rights in his hands," "the pope has, in principle,
taken the place of each bishop."

To reply to these accusations, the German
bishops made a collective declaration in 1875
(The collective declaration is most easily available in English in the appendix of H. Küng's *The
Council, Reform and Reunion*. New York: Sheed
& Ward, 1961) in which they asserted that the
episcopal structure of the Catholic Church has
remained intact and declared that, despite papal
primacy, defined at the Council, Catholic bishops
continue to teach and rule in their diocese as
they always have in the Church. Pope Pius IX
expressed his wholehearted approval of the declaration.

Twenty years later, in his encyclical *Satis
Cognitum* (1896) Pope Leo XIII re-asserted the
episcopal structure of the Church universal.

The encyclical's rather lengthy passage follows:

But if the authority of Peter and his successor is plenary and supreme, it is not to be regarded as the sole authority. For he who made Peter the foundation of the Church also chose twelve whom he called apostles; and just as it is necessary that the authority of Peter be perpetuated in the Roman pontiff, so the bishops who succeed the apostles must inherit their ordinary power. Thus the episcopal order necessarily belongs to the essential constitution of the Church. Although bishops do not receive plenary, universal or supreme authority, they are not to be looked upon as mere representatives of the Roman Pontiffs. They exercise a power truly their own and are ordinary pastors of the people whom they govern (*Satis Cognitum*, §52).

In these citations dealing with episcopal authority, the principal concern is the role of the bishop in his own diocese, and hence, whatever is said about the relationship of pope and episcopacy really refers to the pope's relationship to the individual bishops. It is now common doctrine that the pope has immediate and ordinary jurisdiction in every diocese of the world, and that, at the same time, the local bishop also has immediate and ordinary jurisdiction in the diocese of which he is the pastor. These two jurisdictions in the same territory do not conflict with one another; they do not cancel or inhibit one another, but, on the contrary, they are meant to help and re-enforce one another, making hierarchical authority a more efficient service or ministry to the common good of the faithful. The ultimate force which guarantees the harmonious coordination of the two immediate and ordinary powers in the same diocese is charity. While papal power is supreme and extends over the bishop as well as his flock, the pope must use this power to build up God's kingdom, to foster the life of the diocese and therefore to safeguard the scope of the bishop in the exercise of his pastoral authority.

Looking upon the relationship between papacy and episcopacy in this individual fashion, very little theological advance was made. No theological formula would represent the relationship adequately. By considering only the relation of pope and individual bishop some problems even seem to become more difficult, especially the question concerning the origin of episcopal jurisdiction. Does a bishop receive his ministerial power to teach and rule directly from Christ, or does he receive it directly from the pope? There can be no doubt that in the Church of our day the individual bishop receives his jurisdiction from the Roman pontiff, receives it, in fact, through papal appointment prior to the sacramental consecration. Limiting the whole question to individual bishops and considering the present practice of the Church, it is certainly true to say that the bishop receives his jurisdiction directly from the pope. This was, in fact, the doctrine taught by Pius XII in *Mystici Corporis*, (§41): "(Bishops) enjoy ordinary jurisdictional power granted to them immediately by the pope."

This approach, however, does not give deep insight into the relation of the pope and the world episcopate. Since, in former ages, jurisdic-

tion was not always passed on to bishops through
the successor St. Peter, but also in many other
ways specified by law, we must analyze more profoundly the structure of the Church to determine
the relation between primacy and episcopacy. It
is, in fact, only when we consider the bishops in
their totality that we discover their real place in
the Church of the Lord.

We shall take our lead from canon 228, § 1, of
the Code: "An Ecumenical Council holds supreme power in the universal Church." Here
we learn that the Roman pontiff is not the only
one who exercises supreme authority in the
Church as teacher and ruler, but that the bishops
of the Church united to him in a council also
exercise this supreme power. Conciliar power,
moreover, is not derived from that of the pope.
According to the present legislation, it is true, a
council must be convoked and presided over by
the pope, and its decrees must have papal approval, but once they are promulgated, their
authority is not papal but properly conciliar. If
one were to deny this, the ecumenical councils of
the Church would not hold supreme authority
but simply be consulting boards for the issuing
of papal decrees. It is indeed possible to say that
in a material way the power of the council is derived from the pope, since, according to present
legislation he alone may call it, dissolve it, and
approve its decisions, but formally and theologically, the power of the council is not derived from
that of the pope.

Collegiality of Bishops

The recognition that the bishops as a whole, in

union with their head the pope, can act with supreme authority and bear the charge of the universal Church leads us to the key doctrine determining the relationship between episcopacy and primacy. This doctrine is referred to as "the collegiality of the bishops" or "the unity of the episcopal college." According to this doctrine, the bishops of the Church form a body or college which, as a group, is responsible for teaching and governing the whole people. To understand the meaning of this teaching, we must first consider its biblical foundation.

According to the account of the New Testament, Jesus founded his Church as the new Israel on the twelve Apostles chosen by him. The Twelve were created by Christ as a body. Together they received their instructions (Matt. 10), together they received the call to undertake the mission of the world (Matt. 28, 19), together they were called to be witnesses to the ends of the earth (Acts 1, 8), and together they received the Holy Spirit on the day of Pentecost (Acts 2, 4). We are told that the Apostles received the power of the keys as a group (John 20, 23), and that they are the foundation of the Church (Eph. 2, 20). So great was their sense of unity and their realization that as the Twelve they were the Church's rock, that immediately after the defection of the one, they elected another faithful witness to complete their number (Acts 1, 26). They were conscious that as a body they had received the promise of remaining indefectible: "I shall be with you always" (Matt. 28, 20).

At the same time we also read that Peter, one of the Twelve, was assigned a special place among the Apostles. The promises made to the Apostles as a group were also made to Peter alone. He is the rock; he holds the power of the keys; his mission is indefectible (Matt. 16, 18-19). He is the head of the apostolic college. But it is within this apostolic body to which he inseparably belongs that his office and prerogative must be understood. In other words, the primacy of Peter does not break the unity of the apostolic college as the foundation of the Church of Christ.

According to Catholic faith, the Apostles had successors. These successors were no longer the special instruments of God's self-revelation in Jesus Christ, as were the Apostles, but inasmuch as they preserve, explain and defend the teaching and discipline of the Twelve and, inasmuch as they continue to rule the Church universal, the men who followed the Apostles are called their successors.

These successors of the Apostles are the bishops. This must not be understood as if each bishop can trace his line of consecration back to a single Apostle. What happens, rather, is that the episcopal body as a whole is heir or successor of the apostolic body. The promises which the Lord made to the Twelve and meant to be passed on in his Church are found in the episcopal college as a unit, which is the basic seat of apostolic authority in the Church. The episcopal college, we note, is not the gathering of all Catholic bishops into a single body which sums up the authority which each bishop contributes to it; the episcopal college is, rather, the primary organ of authority in the Church and to be made a bishop means precisely to be integrated into this episcopal college. There, as a member of this college (which as such is the heir of the Twelve), the individual bishop receives his share of apostolic authority to teach and to be a pastor to his flock.

The unity of the episcopal college as heir of the Twelve is the basic theological insight which will solve the questions we have raised in this chapter. The doctrine is ancient but for a number of reasons it has not been taught for several centuries and hence appears rather new to many of our contemporaries. Though not mentioned in the decrees of the First Vatican Council, it is in perfect harmony with them since the primacy of Peter announces his headship within the unity of the episcopal college. The pope has jurisdiction over his brothers, the other bishops, but this supreme jurisdiction does not break the unity of the episcopal body.

Episcopal Jurisdiction

This doctrine throws light on the origin of episcopal jurisdiction. We still say that the pope assigns jurisdiction to the individual bishop, but in the total context of apostolic succession the meaning of this sentence can now be defined with some precision. It is clear, first of all, that the jurisdiction of the episcopal body is not mediated through the pope. It comes directly from Christ. As the pope himself is the successor of St. Peter and receives his ministerial power from the Lord, so is the episcopal college as a whole the successor of the Twelve and receives its ministerial power in the same way. According to Catholic faith, this is unalterable. Neither pope nor council could change this structure. To make the assertion that the jurisdiction of the episcopal college was derived from the plenary power of the pope would be tantamount to saying that Christ has put the total ecclesiastical authority into the hands of Peter and that the other eleven Apostles receive their share from him. Such a theory would go against the teaching of the Scriptures.

How does the individual bishop receive his jurisdiction? He receives his *sacred authority* by being made a member of the episcopal college. He does not receive authority and is then able to join this college but, on the contrary, by being made a member of this college he then shares in the authority which this college as a unity receives from Christ. According to the present legislation, a new member is joined to the episcopal college through the appointment of the pope. In the past this has not always been so. Often a specified number of bishops was able to receive a member into the episcopal college. The Second Vatican Council may declare that fundamentally a bishop is joined to the episcopal college through his sacramental consecration.

But the sacred authority which a bishop receives as a member of the episcopal body is not yet *jurisdiction* in the proper sense, since he must be assigned an area, a territory, or a people in which he can exercise his ministerial authority. The assignment of such an area, a diocese or Church, communicates jurisdiction. Again, according to the legislation of our day, the pope assigns a bishop to a diocese and hence, in this clearly circumscribed sense, we may say that the pope directly imparts jurisdiction to the individual bishop. But he is able to impart this jurisdiction only because the bishop, as a member of the episcopal college, has received a share of the sacred authority which the Twelve have handed on to that body.

Episcopal Co-responsibility

The doctrine of episcopal collegiality also throws light on the function of the individual bishop and his relationship to the pope. It is now no longer simply a question of harmonizing in the same diocese two similar jurisdictions, one of which is supreme. A bishop has a role in the Church which includes more than being the head of his diocese; as a member of the episcopal college he is, at the same, co-responsible for the teaching and shepherding of the universal Church. According to the present legislation, this co-responsibility of the bishops does not find much practical application, but as soon as the Council was convoked the ancient doctrine of episcopal collegiality became again a living reality. At the Council the bishops exercise their office of teachers and legislators for the Church universal in a unique and special manner. Yet we cannot confine this co-responsibility of the bishops for the whole Church to the relatively short periods of ecumenical councils; collegiality is not a privilege bestowed upon the bishops through the pope when calling the council; it is rather a call and duty essentially related to their office.

This understanding of the local bishop may appear new to many. It is, of course, true that the bishop's jurisdiction is confined to his own diocese. But, as a member of the episcopal college, he is concerned with a much vaster part of the Catholic people than his own Church; he is, in fact, concerned with the life of the total Church. His relationship to the pope is not only that of an episcopal subject ruling his diocese in conformity with papal legislation, but as a member of the body of bishops he is an episcopal brother of the pope engaged in dialogue with him.

If the Second Vatican Council wishes to intensify the collegiality of the bishops, a new legislation could create organs through which the co-responsibility we have described could be exercised more freely and more frequently. This could be done, in the first place, through the elevation of episcopal conferences to episcopal assemblies possessing the authority to teach and legislate, subject to the approval of the Holy See. Assigning such power to large groups of bishops would not be an act of legislation inspired simply by pragmatic considerations, but it would correspond profoundly to the very nature of the episcopal office and its collegial coherence. From the most ancient times of the Church it was always believed that the greater the area from which the bishops gathered in councils, the more certain the faithful could be of the Spirit's assistance in their resolutions. To the increasing universality of episcopal councils corresponded an increasing authority attached to them in the teaching of the faith and the imposing of discipline. The general or ecumenical council was the culmination of such episcopal gatherings, and since here the whole episcopate was represented, it was always believed that the Spirit protected his chosen teachers from all error and guaranteed an infallible doctrine.

A second way of intensifying the collegiality of bishops would be the creation of a small council meeting with the pope once a year, a small council composed of bishop-delegates elected by the various regional episcopal conferences, which would deliberate with the supreme head of the Church on matters of teaching and policy. In this way, through their delegates, the bishops of the world would be able to exercise their co-responsibility for the whole Church. Again it should be mentioned that such a small central council would not be a pragmatic institution introduced under the pressure of modern democratic tendencies, but rather an organ of ecclesiastical government corresponding deeply to the divine structure of the Church and revealing the collegial character of episcopacy.

Relationship of Pope and Episcopacy

This leads us to the last question we shall consider in this short essay. Can we define more precisely the relationship of pope and episcopacy? We have said so far that the pope holds supreme authority in the Church both as teacher and law-giver; we have also said that the bishops in union with their head the pope, especially as gathered in an ecumenical council, hold the same supreme authority in the Church. Are there then two relatively distinct subjects of supreme authority in the Church, of which the pope acting alone would be one and the pope acting in union

with his bishops would be the other? This doctrine of the "subjectum duplex supremae auctoritatis" was indeed taught by many theologians.
It was taught by several great 19th-century
theologians, such as Kleutgen, Schrader and
Scheeben, and from the minutes of the working
commission at the First Vatican we know that
the definition of papal primacy was not meant
to prejudge the doctrine of the "subjectum duplex" (See J. P. Torrell, *La Theologie de l'Epis-
copat au premier concile du Vatican*, Paris 1961,
pp. 149-58). In our own day the doctrine of the
"subjectum duplex supremae auctoritatis" has
found many supporters.

This doctrine has the advantage that it brings
to light the dialogue structure within the exercise of supreme authority in the Church. According to this doctrine there is one single and
undivided supreme authority granted by Christ
to the Church, which is exercised either by the
pope alone or, at other times, by the totality of
the bishops including their head, the pope. The
weakness of the doctrine is, however, that the
"either/or" in the exercise of this authority does
not bring out the organic character of the
Church's unity nor does it show that the supreme
authority of the pope leaves intact and serves the
unity of the episcopal college. It creates the impression that the pope acting as the supreme
head of the Church places himself outside of the
episcopal college to which, in fact, he inseparably
belongs as the principal member.

Against the accusation, often raised against
the teaching of the First Vatican, that the pope's
primacy severs him from the rest of the Church

and especially from the bishops, and thus makes him an independent and therefore arbitrary ruler, we must assert quite vigorously that the pope acts within the Church and more especially within the body of bishops. Even when defining doctrine "ex sese, non ex consensu Ecclesiae" the pope remains the principal member of this body and exercises his power in the name of, and in favor of, the whole body of bishops to whom Christ has assigned the universal government of the Church.

We prefer not to speak, therefore, of a twofold subject of supreme authority in the Church. Another doctrinal position is at present taught by many theologians and has been adopted by a great number of bishops, according to which there is *one single* seat of supreme authority in the Church, and this is the episcopal college. As heir of the Twelve (including Peter) it is supreme in teaching and ruling. The exercise of this supreme power may take place in various ways, but each time the whole episcopal college is in some sense involved. Sometimes the bishops exercise their supreme power in union with their head, the pope, at an ecumenical council. At other times the bishops teach or act in union with the pope while remaining dispersed over the world. At other times again, the pope himself teaches or legislates with supreme authority for the universal Church, but when he does so he exercises the supreme authority given to the episcopal body which he, as its head, is able to use *ex sese*, of his own accord. This means that the pope exercising supreme power, while not dependent on the consent of the Church or of the bishops, always acts in the name of the body of bishops and, as it were, for them, in their favor. Without the slightest detriment to the pope's supreme position as defined by the First Vatican, this understanding of the unity and primacy of the episcopal college places papal primacy into an ecclesiological context in which the pope appears more clearly as a member of the Church, a bishop of a diocese, and as head of the whole Church exercising his supreme office as a ministry in the apostolic body of bishops for the good of all the Christian faithful.

9

The Church Expecting Christ's Return

Mother M. Chabanel

PERE CONGAR is of the opinion that Vatican Council I gave theology something of a charter when it pointed out that the best way to "arrive at a very fruitful understanding of the mysteries" was to take into consideration the "links that the mysteries have with each other and with *the destiny of man*" (Denz. 1796). In these words the Council restored theology to the great Christian tradition. One mystery important for an understanding of the Church which has thus been recovered is that of eschatology. No longer is it thought of as an isolated treatise dealing exclusively with the four "last things" by which the individual will pay the penalty of debt to divine justice. True, it is the mystery of the end, the *eschaton*, but the end essentially linked with the great redemptive act of Christ. Within its perspective, the Church's doctrine concerning

91

the "last things" is set in its true light, and the mystery of the Church herself is illumined.

The intermediate stage in which the Church finds herself now only derives its true meaning from its relationship to the final stage. In the reality of the end, the Christian recognizes with joy his communal vocation to the Church, and is strengthened accordingly to move steadfastly forward with the people of God to its fulfillment. But this is not all. Within the theological perspective of the *eschaton* one realizes that the Church is still only in the earthly, temporal, and hence imperfect stage of her existence. The laws of this stage are those of growth, development, progress, as the Gospel parables illustrate. One cannot then regard Christ's gift as totally realized, nor can one belittle the reality of the mysterious possession of it now. To understand the tension between the present and the future is the function of a true eschatology.

Object of the Church's Hope

The Church is always concerned with three-dimensional time: she looks to the past, when, as God's people, she became in Christ the inheritor of the promise of Israel; she lives in the present where "possessing the first-fruits of the Spirit" she shares through Christ, and in him, the life of the triune God; she longs for the future when her tribulations of these days en route to the heavenly Jerusalem will be crowned with the glory of her Lord, and God will be all in all. As Body seeking greater identity with the Head, or as Bride longing for greater union with her Spouse, it is the future, naturally enough,

that claims her deepest concern, for in the light
of Christ's final coming she sees her whole history.

Conscious that she is the new Israel called
by the Spirit to be holy with the holiness of the
eternal Son, she is, nevertheless, aware that the
pattern of Israel's life is in many respects her
own; she, too, is the people of the Exodus, a
people on pilgrimage through the desert of this
world to the land of promise. Then only shall
she possess the fullness of her inheritance.
Christ's glorious Easter triumph is a fact; her
share in it, however, is not complete. She must
struggle against sin, which, though no longer
invincible, still menaces her. Its tyranny, though
undermined by Christ's first coming, will only
collapse completely at his second coming. At
that time, God, by a cosmic event, will intervene
to round off the history of the world. Though
it refers to a material event, this eschatology is
a divine mystery, the final act in the design of
God's love, and one which the Church longs for,
rejoices at, and never ceases to hope for.

Christian and Eschatological Hope

She keeps this eschatological hope ever before her children, inviting them to ponder this
act of God's all-wise and merciful plan, to know
it, so that by ordering their lives aright, they
may enter into it and profit by it. There are
several areas of Christian thinking to which
eschatology makes a significant contribution. It
is a source of security to the insecure: Christ is
the Lord of history—"be still and know that I
am God," he says in Psalm 45 (46). It restores

the sense of community to Christian spirituality: the eschatological kingdom is promised—not to an isolated individual, but to the new people of God, forming one Body with Christ, the Church. It corrects an excessive and exclusive preoccupation with saving one's soul: Christ's redemptive act includes not merely the spiritual but the temporal aspects of one's life. It shows the Christian how to love this world, for everything in it that is loved legitimately will pass over into eternity; the foundation of its reconciliation has been laid (Col. 1, 16-20); the cornerstone has been placed in position forever. A true eschatological outlook, then, builds up a healthy Christian, at once detached and confident, patient and alert, whom the Lord when he comes will find watching.

This brief essay, however, is concerned with the role of eschatology in the study of the Church. In this area, eschatological hope is the magnetic north to which all integral ecclesiology must be pointed. This is so for two reasons: first, only in the *eschaton* can Christians reconcile the tension between the Church's present reality and her future ideal; and secondly, only in the *eschaton* can they integrate the two apparently contradictory principles of the holiness of the Church and the sinfulness of her members.

Paradox of the Imperiled and the Assured

A Christian's view of the Church will be enlarged by setting it in the perspective of eternity. The Church, the people of God, both pastors and faithful, committed to a furthering of the reign of God in this world, understand the foundation of their supernatural hope—the return in glory of their Lord, the resurrection of the body, the re-creation of the whole cosmos by the Spirit. But the final reign of God, the complete triumph of peace and justice can only be established on the ruins of this world. Christians seem to belong to two ages simultaneously. They share in the divine riches now, they have already laid hold of them by grace, and yet they are still unfulfilled, expecting the kingdom of glory. St. Paul insists that the Christian in his present life participates in Christ's risen life, but since he is not risen himself, this participation is hidden and mysterious (Cerfaux, *The Church in the Theology of St. Paul,* Herder & Herder, New York).

This tension between the "already" and the "not yet" makes us realize that many aspects of the earthly Church are only provisional. Hence, it is not in her juridical and utilitarian aspects that the Church invites her children to have faith. She knows that her hierarchic and sacramental principles, which are the instruments of her growth and a sharing in the earthly condition of her members, will one day be abandoned as "mortal and historical clothing" (de Lubac, *Splendour of the Church,* Paulist Press, New York). She invites her children to have faith in Christ, in his irreversible and total triumph in which they shall one day share. Her limited successes and many apparent defeats in these days are merely approaches to this triumph. In her liturgy she is at pains to remind her children that she is on the way. During the Easter Vigil she experiences and sums up the meaning of her long journey through history, her Exodus. Freed from Egypt, she lives now in the desert, and makes her way through it, not without conflict. But because Christ has come, she knows that he will come again, being himself the *Eschaton*.

Paradox of the Holy and the Unholy

To belong to this Church which announces Christ's return is not at all restful. God's Word tells us of the bitter conflict between the reign of God and the reign of God's adversary (Congar, *The Mystery of the Temple*, Newman Press, Westminster, Md.). In this struggle the Christian is troubled once again by the curious paradox of his condition: he belongs to a Church that is holy, yet the Church he belongs to is made up of men like himself who are sinners. The Church is holy because she is in Christ. While the crucified and risen Jesus shares with his Church the fullness of his holiness, his disciples may still be found guilty together (Baum, *Progress and Perspectives*, Sheed & Ward, New York). The disciples are in a continual struggle with the powers of darkness. In them and around them sin tries to deny God's plan of love. They carry the treasure of God's grace in fragile vessels, bearing within themselves a frightening potential for sin. A precarious balance exists between the certitude of our possessing Christ and the consciousness of never measuring up to the ideal proposed to us.

Eschatological hope can become a singularly difficult virtue, but within its perspective the Christian finds grounds for patience. Sin delays the coming of Christ, but repentance hastens it.

The Church in her liturgy constantly invites her children to surrender themselves to the work of purification which Christ wishes to accomplish in them. Sin is the cause of all mediocrity, futility, divisiveness in the Church; penitence is the Christian's great hope of overcoming it in order to cooperate in the final triumph of God's people. In Christ, the *Eschaton*, their sinfulness will be totally transformed by the holiness of the Church.

By thus revealing the deepest meaning of the Church, eschatology has opened up an area of fruitful dialogue. Many theologians, de Lubac, Cerfaux, Congar and Thils, to mention only four, have already enriched the discussion by their happy faculty of linking the mystery of eschatology with that of the Church, and both of them to the destiny of man. The deliberations of Vatican Council II, especially those concerning the Church, will undoubtedly reflect the flowering of this theology restored to the great Christian tradition.

10
Prayer
for Christian Unity

Paul Broadhurst

THE prayer of Christ that all may be one appears in the heart of the eucharistic liturgy. At the beginning of the eucharistic prayer, and again before the communion we ask that God may unite his Church—"adunare" and "coadunare" are the words used by the Roman Missal. Catholics believe, and irreformably so, that the Church of Christ is already one and possesses the basic unity which he himself has bestowed upon his people. Yet this unity must be constantly activated so as to engage each member of God's people in the fullness of the gifts he has bestowed upon them. Unity is not only a gift but also a task, a task for whose accomplishment Christ has sent his Holy Spirit.

The Church's unity suffers from the lack of charity among her members. Her unity suffers, moreover, from the tragic situation in which men baptized in Christ and united to him in faith belong to separate communities. Praying for the unity of the Church, then, means calling upon the Holy Spirit to inspire all men reborn in her baptism and liberated by her Gospel to enter fully upon the unity which is God's gift to his people.

The importance of Christian unity today leads us to extend our prayer for unity beyond its occurrence in the liturgy. Surely, the first step in bringing Christ's prayer for unity to fruition is the union of all Christians in common prayer, beseeching the Holy Spirit to gather them ever more completely into the unity of the Body of Christ. Such a prayer is a manifestation of a real, though initial unity.

Two distinct movements of prayer for unity have arisen among Catholics in our own time. The first, started by Father Paul Watson, is now carried on by the Franciscan Friars of the Atonement. The other, originated by Abbé Paul Couturier, is promoted today by the center "Unité Chrétienne" at Lyons in France. The difference between these two movements can be described quite readily.

The prayers for unity advocated by the Friars of the Atonement, especially in connection with the "Chair of Unity Octave," seek unity through prayer by referring to the visible structure of the Roman Church. We pray that separated Christians may be converted or reconciled to the Church built upon Peter. By stating our intentions in this way, however, we make it impossible for Protestants and Orthodox Christians to join us in prayer, for it would be sinful for a man to pray for what he does not recognize to be the will of God. While the Friars of the Atonement regret that dissident Christians are unable to join us in this prayer, they feel that fidelity to Catholic doctrine demands that we express our creed explicity in prayer and dispel any doubts of separated Christians that we seek a unity which is not in continuity with the Catholic Church.

The second movement, flourishing in France and many other countries of Europe and now directed by Père Michalon, words its prayer for unity in such a way that separated Christians may more easily join Catholics in their intercession. This group believes that the one Church of Christ is built on Peter and the Twelve, but realizing that the Church is a mystery of grace, it feels the unity we seek may be expressed in terms of the spiritual gifts that are communicated to us in the Church. The intention suggested by the center "Unité Chrétienne" for the Week of Universal Prayer for Christian Unity, as they call it, is "the unity which Christ desires by the means he desires." They do not indicate that the object of our prayer is the return of others to the Church of Rome; rather, they plead for the sanctification of Catholics, for the sanctification of Orthodox, Anglicans and Protestants.

Christians separated from Rome gladly join in these prayers. Catholics, of course, praying in this way believe that the sanctification that God offers to men is totally available only in the Church whose center is at Rome. Only there, they are convinced, are all the gifts of Christ present to us. But because this aspect of our creed is only implicit, and not expressly mentioned, Christians separated from us can join in the prayer for the unity which is Christ's will for his people.

The Catholic Position

Protestants have repeatedly asked Catholics to clarify their own position on prayer for Christian unity. Is it, or is it not possible, they wish to know, to organize a week of common prayer in which all Christians desiring unity may take part? Writing in the July, 1962 issue of *The Ecumenical Review*, Lukas Vischer, research secretary of Faith and Order, asks that the Second Vatican Council clarify the Church's position in regard to common prayer for unity.

It would seem, however, that this is not the kind of question that requires an official decision. The position of the Catholic Church is already quite clear on this matter. And yet it is true, and most unfortunate, that a controversy has arisen between the two Catholic movements of prayer, the "Chair of Unity Octave" and the "Week of Universal Prayer for Christian Unity." Such a controversy tends to make a dogmatic issue of something that is at most a different approach to prayer for unity.

In truth, the Catholic Church prays for Christian unity in many ways. In some of her prayers she tends to emphasize that unity will be brought about by the will of Christ through the power of the Holy Spirit. In others, she emphasizes the visible manifestations which she believes will embody the fruition of Christ's will for unity, namely, the sacramental and hierarchical structure of the Church. She does not claim these two ways of prayer are mutually exclusive. In their expression both ways of prayer tend to emphasize a single aspect of the unity desired, but they in no way exclude each other.

The liturgy usually expresses the unity we desire in terms of God's will for his people. In the newly renamed *Mass for Christian Unity*, for instance, we ask God "to pour down upon the Christian people the grace of union" and "to grant that all may be united to the true Shepherd of the Church." These words echo the Lord's prayer "that all may be one."

The Popes and Prayer for Unity

In recent decades the popes have exhibited different tendencies in their prayer for unity, depending on their interpretation of the needs of the day. Leo XIII often defined the unity we seek in terms of Scripture and liturgy, asking all separated Christians to join Catholics in the prayer for Christian unity (*cf.* Gregory Baum, *That They May Be One*, Newman, 1958, p. 132). On the other hand, Pius XII preferred to pray, in the last years of his pontificate, that separated Christians might recognize the Lord's promises made to Peter and his successors.

Pope John XXIII's statements have reflected both approaches. His general prayer intentions published in the first year of his reign included the following: "that the Christian faithful may ceaselessly implore the help of the Holy Spirit in restoring the union of all Christians in one true faith and Church." This emphasis is found in many documents of John XXIII. It reveals a sensitive awareness that to depict union only in terms of a return of all Christians to Rome would vastly oversimplify the matter.

To speak of "return" divorced from other dimensions of Christian unity, suggests to Protestants a reversion to the 16th century and a replay of the old debates. In reality, the theological issues have greatly changed since that day. The Catholic Church has undergone a renewal at the Council of Trent and looks forward to a second renewal through the Second Vatican Council. These vital issues do not reverberate in the words "return to the Mother Church."

In his encyclical convoking the Second Vatican Council, *Ad Petri Catholicam*, July 2, 1959, Pope John expressed his hope that dissident Christians be inspired "to seek out that unity which Jesus Christ prayed for so ardently from his heavenly Father." In other documents, however, Pope John leans toward the other, the more concrete way of designating Christian unity.

Each of these two ways of signifying the unity we seek is, then, legitimate. We may pray that God's will shall triumph in the unity of his people, or that the promises which the Lord made to the visible society of his founding shall be fulfilled. The conflict between the "Chair of Unity Octave" and the "Week of Universal Prayer for Christian Unity" is not a profound one, since it is in no way based on a doctrinal difference, and hence we cannot expect the teaching authority in the Church to settle the matter for us. As Catholics, we must learn to transcend the present terms of conflict and meet on a deeper level of theological understanding from which the original positions appear in a new light.

Ecumenical Approach

What, then, are the principles which make our prayer for Christian unity truly Catholic as well as ecumenical?

1. While we may refer in prayer for unity to the Church's visible structure, to the papacy, the apostolic hierarchy or the seven sacraments, we must clearly announce that these elements are not ends in themselves, but serve and mediate the unity of men in Christ. We must avoid speaking of Christian unity as if it were merely the work of men, as if it were something merely organizational in nature. The expression of our prayer for unity should always make clear that the unity for which we hope is the work of the Holy Spirit.

2. The terms of our prayer should suggest that we Catholics too must be willing to change. While we may refer to the change of mind needed in Christians separated from us, we must make it clear that we recognize our own need for renewal. We should avoid speaking of Christian unity as if it involved on our part only patiently waiting for others to act.

3. In our time, when all Christians desire to pray together for the unity that their one Lord desires for his Church, Catholics can find nothing in their faith to prevent them from joining with Orthodox and Protestants in a prayer for unity that would be acceptable to the consciences of all concerned. For all recognize that unity will be the work of the Spirit of Christ, and will demand from all a renewal, sometimes painful, of their Christianity. All can join without reservation in a prayer for unity that expresses these truths.

11

A Catholic Interpretation of History

Gregory Baum

SINCE the topic of the origin and development of values in human civilization is intimately connected with the reflection on human history, it is of special concern to the theologian. For it is only through biblical faith that history has become the object of reflection. Only through biblical faith did history tell a meaningful story, one which man had to listen to in order to understand himself. In non-biblical cultures, the man of wisdom sought to penetrate the contingent, and hence the historical, to discover the lasting and necessary behind the shifting scene of events; the movement of wisdom constantly transcended historical existence to eternal verities. To be in history was really a pity. Opinion, and not science, was the kind of knowledge that could be drawn from man's historical existence.

This lack of appreciation of history is not surprising, since it was impossible for the ancient philosophers to give a meaningful interpretation of historical events. A philosopher may enlarge his view, he may take in long stretches of time and vast areas of human culture, but he is never certain whether this circle has encompassed all that is significant. Since he constantly suspects that what he studies is only a section of human culture, he will not dare to discuss its orientation. In such a case, meaning is not in history, but in being saved from history. In order to say anything significant about history and its movement, we must have a point transcending history from which to judge it. We must know the beginning and the end of the historical process, or at least know that it has a beginning and an end. For this reason it was the revelation of God in Israel that enabled men to reflect on history.

The revelation of the meaning of history is not incidental to the religion of the Bible; it stands at its very core. There God reveals himself as the Lord of mercy who has created men in order to join them to himself in friendship. While men are stubborn and selfish, always breaking the unity of the divine plan, God intervenes in the course of history to form them into a people, *his* people, to redirect their lives to a concern for others, and to liberate them for what is best in themselves. God reveals himself so that we may know who we are and what is the meaning of our history.

According to the Bible, God is the Lord of history. He directs it as he wishes. At the same time it is man who through his decisions, through the answers he gives to his God, makes history. History is both the locus of divine self-revelation and the creation of man's free decisions. And yet, because even man's freedom is in the hands of the Lord who made him, we know that history will end well: God will see to it that men will be reconciled to him as his holy people.

From the Judaeo-Christian faith, the conviction that history possesses a destiny, or that historical developments are progressive realizations of a plan, has deeply penetrated Western culture. These ideas have not always entered men's minds through the Church's preaching or through reading the Bible, but whether in line with Christian thought or in opposition to it, the notion of history as having a beginning and a direction, as fulfilling a law and simultaneously as being the locus of human decisions—all this has completely conquered the mind of man. Christianity has taught Western man to be self-conscious about history, not to regard it as an accidental sequence of events, but to study its coherence and interpret its orientation.

Secularization of Christian Hope

The 19th-century ideals of evolution and progress were related to biblical faith; but because these theories were created in reaction to conservative religious forces and inspired by humanistic ideals of various kinds, they were basically secularist in outlook, positing a law of development, immanent to history itself. Whether we look at Auguste Comte, who believed that the progress of science would deliver mankind from its enemies and produce a new world, or at Karl

Marx, who regarded a necessary sociological dia-
lectic as the inevitable force leading mankind to
the perfect society, we are witnessing a faith in
history which is nothing but the secularization of
Christian hope. Yet if any theory of human progress regards this progress as wholly immanent to
humanity itself, it will lose the dimension which
has given meaning to history in the first place,
namely the free decision of God, and hence will
ultimately destroy progress. Thus the Comtean
understanding of progress has led to an empty
scientism which has closed men's eyes to what is
deepest in them and therefore removed the terms
in which progress can be measured, and the
Marxian ideal of the dialectical progress of history has been usurped as an instrument of power
politics and made to serve in the conflict of
nations.

Despite these deformations the conviction of
history as direction, as progress, remains unchal-
lenged in Western civilization and even the nations of Asia and Africa have caught this spirit
from us. They have come to believe in their mission as nations. They now think of themselves as
having a contribution to make; they regard our
times as "their hour," the propitious moment of
their self-realization. History for them is no
longer that which is suffered, but that in which
they are actively engaged in order to change
themselves and modify history.

There may be comparatively few Christians in
the world; yet their understanding of history has
once and for all caught the minds of men, to be
preserved or corrupted, never to be lost. Man has
become conscious that he is the master of nature,

that he belongs to an order superior to the world that surrounds him, and that he can manipulate the forces of nature by science and technology to serve his own ends. In the great non-biblical cultures man stood over against nature contemplating its beauty. For them nature gave expression to a cosmic law, to the divine order of things, and man reached his perfection by submitting to the inner harmony of the world of nature. The cosmos was a more perfect image of the divine than was man. In the Scriptures, on the contrary, man is created as the master of creation, destined to know it, to transform it, and to build society. Man, according to the biblical vision, does not submit to the cosmos; while he realizes that his surroundings are largely a given thing which he has not chosen, he is continually called to make decisions which affect his environment and initiate its transformation.

In this limited sense, the world has become Christian. No doubt, this advance remains ambiguous, to be used for good or evil; but the notion of history as destiny has completely transformed our civilization.

Human Dignity in Historical Aspect

The understanding of history as development is related to another value, central in Western civilization, which is derived from biblical revelation, that is, the peculiar dignity of the human person. The men of wisdom of ancient Greece preferred to think of man in terms of his "nature," in terms of what all men have in common, the soul and body, the faculties of intellect and will; and man's involvement in time appeared to them as a contingent or accidental factor. In the Bible, however, man is essentially related to the historical order. It belongs to his essence to be in history. Man is constantly facing a situation which is determined by the past and called upon to enter into a future partially created by his own decision. This freedom of man to transcend the given-ness of each situation by an action which embodies his own decision and transforms his environment is precisely what makes history possible. Animals do not have history. Their lives are determined by impulses. But the essence of man implies the need to decide for himself, and it is only by means of these decisions that he comes to be what he is. Without them he remains a child.

By this freedom (from which God's action in us is not excluded!) we are distinct from the rest of the cosmos, superior to it, belonging to a different order of being. Man is not one object among the many objects of the world; he is a subject, reflecting and making decisions which transform him as well as his surroundings.

This understanding of the human person is of biblical origin; in the Bible we are told that man is created in the image and likeness of God. Man is not an object in the world, but a subject, one who can engage in dialogue with God, the supreme Subject. It is quite true that according to the scriptural account man has lost, through a disloyalty in which the whole race is involved, his freedom and power positively to respond to God, but we are also told that through God's redeeming Word addressed to Israel and finally sent to all men in Jesus Christ, we are set free again to acknowledge God's call and become again, in the true sense, the image of God, the supreme Person.

This understanding of the dignity of the person has profoundly influenced Western thought. Christian and non-Christian thinkers of the West have been overwhelmed by the grandeur of man, despite his failures and his malice. It was especially the Protestant Reformation which brought the realization of the uniqueness of man's freedom to the conscience of the common man, first in Europe and then in America. But here again it it only in a truly Christian context that this personalism does not deteriorate into a self-seeking individualism. The person is not meant to be the center of his own conscious life. If we set ourselves up as the end of our own personal history, we caricature the order of the world and fall into blinding selfishness. What it means to be a person we are taught profoundly only by God, who addresses us in his Word, and it is in this same Word that we find ourselves belonging to a plan of salvation which embraces the whole people of God. In the Christian message we learn that the dimensions of our freedom are the worship of God and the service of others. We discover ourselves as persons when we love our neighbor.

Despite our hypocrisy, our greed, our injustices, and our crimes, the possibility of progress and the freedom of the human person in love have entered modern human consciousness, probably never to be erased. However much we sin against these insights now, modern civilization is profoundly marked by these Christian values.

Universal Character of Salvation-History

When I attribute these values to biblical revelation, I do not wish to belittle the contribution
which human thought and the experience of
mankind have made to their discoveries. The
Christian believes that the Lord of his faith is
the Lord of the world and that, therefore, he has
not only left an inkling of his plan in the hearts
of all men but also, and especially, continues to
act in the cultural and religious aspirations of all
peoples. While we believe that salvation-history
is restricted to Israel and the Christian Church,
in the sense that only there do men realize the
merciful ways of God with the world, in a wider
sense salvation-history pervades the history of
all peoples, especially since the coming of Christ.
The growing self-realization of man and the unification of the human race, of which we find a
beginning in Greek philosophy and many developments in the wisdom of all ages (and more
particularly in the aspirations of vast numbers of
men in our day) are not unrelated to the initiative of God in the world. Even if men claim that
they have discovered these values by reason
alone, or by experience or direct intuition, this
does not exclude it being the God of history
having declared in Christ his universal will to
save, who is acting in their spirits. In the understanding of the Christian message, therefore,
Christians have always learned from those outside the Church to whom God has given insight,
however incomplete.

I wish to stress this point. Declaring that the
scriptural faith is the source of cultural values
does not mean that from the beginning these

values were consciously seized upon by the Christian community. It is rather through the experience of many centuries, when Christians were obliged to put new questions to the Word of God, that much of what this Word contains came to light and produced explicit knowledge. Here are some instances. When America and other lands across the seas were discovered in the 15th century, Christians reflected on the Gospel in order to find a moral standard applicable to Christians and non-Christians alike. The rise of Marxism in the 19th century urged Christians to seek anew in the Christian message the meaning of society and mutual responsibility, and the advance of science and technology have forced Christians to question again God's message regarding the meaning and purpose of the cosmos. The ideas of history as evolution and the human person as unique are derived from the Scriptures, but in the process of their clarification the whole of human experience has been involved, if not with positive insights, then at least with new questions.

I am tempted to go a step further. When the Christian community was blind to values or ideals contained in the Gospel, God sent them prophets and saints to remind them; but when the Christian people preferred their comfortable ignorance, God would permit that the yearning for this neglected value would leap beyond the borders of the Church, there to kindle a movement seeking to establish it in society. But because this movement was outside the Church it suffered from the unprotectedness of human life and though its purpose was good, it embraced erroneous ideas, became hostile to the Christian Gospel and ultimately initiated its own destruction. Is not most of the post-Christian belief in Western culture, and especially Marxism, a reaction of this kind? Were there not Christian values, neglected in the Church, which caught the hearts of men outside the Church, but in their minds did not these values become secularized and turned against the Church and perhaps even against man? Was not the Enlightenment something which Christians should have carried out? Was not the intention of the French revolution something for which Christians should have worked? Were not the ideals of Marxism aims for which Christians should have labored? But we were slow to act and God permitted the movement to go on elsewhere, caught up in errors, to become a reproach to us.

As a Roman Catholic, I would extend this interpretation of history by saying that schisms in the Church have been produced in similar ways. Because we did not live up to the ideals of the Gospel and heed the prophets sent to the Church, God permitted that these evangelical values stirred men up to begin movements outside the Church and partially against her, standing in judgment over her negligence. And yet these movements of reaction, being unprotected, became subject to distortions and self-destructive tendencies.

The Christian message of selflessness and love contradicts the human inclination on one level. But because the message which God spoke into the world is in harmony *on a deeper level* with human aspirations of which the same God is the author, many, if not most Christians believe that there are certain norms of human behavior, certain moral ideals, which are common to all human beings whether they are believers or not. The history of human thought testifies to this. The Stoic philosophers spoke of a natural law, and immanent *logos*, to which men must submit to find wisdom and happiness; and the philosophers of the Enlightenment spoke of natural laws of human behavior, determined by reason, which have universal validity. The formulations of these laws were often at variance, and the grounds for their validity depended on the various systems of philosophy; but they do give witness to the common conviction of mankind that there are common standards of behavior for all men. Some Protestant thinkers deny any kind of "natural law," but when one analyzes their thought their denial is often simply a rejection of any one formulation of these abiding norms or a protest against the idea that man can find a moral ideal by following the bent of his nature, without God's grace.

Most Christians, Protestant and Catholic, believe that there are constants of human behavior, certain common aspirations of what is deepest in man (and therefore in contact with God) beyond any of the formulated systems of natural law, an inclination produced in the human heart by the God who rules the destiny of men toward their salvation. These constants of human behavior can serve as the basis of understanding and cooperation for all men. These basic values are precisely *the dignity of the human person and the possibility of progress in society*, to which these persons

are linked. Both the person and the common good
are supreme values. In various periods of history,
depending on the self-awareness of men and the
evolution of society, the interrelation between
the person and the common good was expressed
in different sets of laws and institutions, and in
this sense we may well speak of an evolution of
morality. But behind this development stands
the common conviction that man is free and that
this freedom implies responsibility to serve the
community in which alone the freedom of all is
assured.

As a Christian I am very conscious that moral
insight or the acknowledgment of these values is
due to divine initiative. It is due to God in a
direct way through his message addressed to the
Church, but it is also due to him, less visibly,
through his influence on the hearts of men seeking the right order of the universe. The so-called
natural law, therefore, is not based on some definition of human nature, nor on the power of
man's reason, nor on the inner harmony of the
cosmos, but through man's nature and intelli-
gence, conditioned by his goodwill, on the movement of God in history reconciling humanity with
himself.

Unity of Mankind

This leads me to the last question I wish to
raise in this brief essay. Do Christians believe in
historical progress? Do we believe that the promises which God has made to Israel and which
have been fulfilled in Jesus Christ are meant to
transform this historical existence of ours, lead
men into the concord of one human family, and

unify and humanize our life on earth? Here the answer is not easy. All Christians teach that God's action in history draws men to salvation and holiness, preparing them for *the age to come*, and all accept the existence of another force in history, the mystery of evil, the power of human negation which has been with us from the beginning and will remain with us till the end of time. Is it therefore possible to say that the direction of human history is toward greater self-realization? The answer cannot be given from a study of human civilizations, for all apparent progress in this world remains ambiguous. Even the unification of mankind, the humanization and interconnectedness of human life which we witness in our age could be the preparation of a universal revolt against God, a denial of the divine and hence, ultimately, of the truly human. If there is an answer to the question of progress in history, it must, again, be given from a point outside of history.

There are an increasing number of Christian writers in our day, in the Catholic Church and in other Churches, who take so seriously the incarnation of God in Christ, that is, the personal and irrevocable union of God with the human nature of Jesus, that they feel that God has linked himself once and for all to human history. These theologians would appeal to God's universal will to save, revealed in Christ, to the perfect self-surrender of Christ on the cross and the universality of his victory over death and evil, in order to assert that, with the coming of Christ, something irreversible has happened in human history. The whole history of mankind has been reoriented toward reconciliation with God. These theologians would say, therefore, that it is the mission of the Church to serve humanity in its needs on this earth, to inspire men to find and foster the values common among themselves, and to collaborate in the building of the earthly city, so that the will of God, which is peace and unity, will become more manifest in this world. These writers, then, rejecting the secularistic understanding of progress which has characterized the 19th century, and overcoming the inclination to despair so common in modern philosophy, confidently assert that God has established an historical movement in Jesus Christ which is destined to unify and pacify men on this earth.

Reading Pope John's encyclical letter *Pacem in Terris*, addressed to all men of goodwill, one has the impression that this was the vision of the Pope. He believed that it is the mission of the Church to serve the unity of mankind.

Part III

ECUMENICAL
DEVELOPMENTS

12

The Catholic Church and the W.C.C.

Gregory Baum

A T the *Faith and Order Conference*, Montreal, 1963, the question was asked several times why the Catholic Church—or, as she was called there, the Roman Catholic Church—does not belong to the World Council of Churches. While the question did not belong to the central preoccupations of the Montreal Conference it recurred on the margin of the important discussions on unity.

The World Council of Churches is a fellowship of Christian Churches which, together, through dialogue and common action, seek the unity which is God's gift to his people. The W.C.C. is not, and does not intend to become, a super-Church or a substitute for the *Una Sancta* announced in the Creed. It is an instrumental community of, and for, the Churches enabling them to come together on a footing of equality to discuss, to study one another, to collaborate on various projects, to strive for greater unity, and to manifest in visible fashion the unity which is theirs already. Is there a reason why the Catholic Church should not belong to the Council?

No Dogmatic Obstacles

The Toronto Declaration of 1950, spelling out in detail what the W.C.C. was and wanted to be, made it quite clear that "the W.C.C. is not based on any particular conception of the Church." The Declaration states: "The Council does not prejudge the ecclesiological problem. Membership in the W.C.C. does not imply that a Church treats its own conception of the Church as merely relative. Membership in the Council does not imply that each Church must regard the other members as Churches in the true and full sense of the word." All that is required is that a Church joining the Council acknowledge in the other member Churches elements of the true Church, *i.e.*, regard them as being, in some sense, ecclesial realities.

On this basis the Orthodox Churches had been able to become members of the W.C.C. Since the Catholic Church also claims to be the one true Church but is willing to acknowledge in other Churches life-giving sacramental and doctrinal elements of the Gospel, and hence regard them as ecclesial realties, there would seem to be no dogmatic reason why she could not belong to the W.C.C.

Is the Toronto Declaration of 1950 still a statement describing the nature and character of the W.C.C.? Many developments have taken place since that time. At New Delhi great progress was made in defining a common concept of Church unity so that it is no longer true to say, as does the Toronto Declaration, that the W.C.C. is not based on any particular concept of the Church. Even apart from the New Delhi statement on Christian unity, many things have happened in the World Council. Its membership has greatly increased. It comprises today a greater variety of Churches than it did in 1950. The International Missionary Council has been integrated into the World Council. New areas of cooperation, of common missionary action and of joint witness have been gained. The question has arisen in the minds of many theologians of the W.C.C. whether the character of this Council has not undergone an evolution.

Some of these theologians wish to speak of the Council as possessing, in some sense, an ecclesial character. They insist that the Council performs functions which are, more or less, ecclesiastical. While the Council has no doctrine, no sacraments, and no ministry, it does give common witness to Christ in the world, exerts a certain teaching ministry among Christians, serves the needs of the world in spiritual and material ways, and encourages worship. It seems to some that the Council has become so important in the Christian world that a Church claiming to be catholic and ecumenical can no longer afford to remain aloof from it. The Council has become, in the eyes of influential World Council theologians, "an aspect of the total mystery of the Church." This might mean that the catholicity and unity which Christ has given to his people are enbodied in the W.C.C. to such a degree that apart from it no Church can claim to possess catholicity and unity in perfect obedience to Christ.

Such formulations are not likely to please a Church that regards itself as institutionally perfect, *i.e.* that regards itself as having been created through the institutional gifts of the Lord (Gospel teachings, sacraments, apostolic orders), even if its use of these unfailing gifts should be imperfect. It is for this reason that the Orthodox Churches opposed any tendency at Montreal to attribute an ecclesial character to the World Council and, thanks to their protest, the report of the Montreal Conference does not really go further than the Toronto Declaration in defining the character of the World Council.

Christians, of course, have no difficulty in acknowledging the action of God in, and through, the World Council. God's merciful dealings are not confined to his sacramental Church. But to claim that the W.C.C. is part of the present *Heilsgeschichte* in such a way that whoever remains aloof from it thereby withdraws from the total order through which God works in the world, is more than Catholics could admit. On the other hand, if God, the Lord of history, calls together his faithful people through the World Council, the Christian theologian must indeed reflect on the meaning of the Council in God's redemptive design. The Council is more than a shop or an office; it has proven itself to be a place where God speaks of unity and fidelity to the Churches.

Several Practical Obstacles

There are several practical reasons why the Catholic Church has not joined the World Council of Churches. It is my personal opinion that one of these is the fear of confusing Christians—Protestant, Orthodox and Catholic. Until now, the Catholic Church has remained aloof from organized movements for unity to manifest her own faith that she is the authentic heir of the apostolic community. Until now, Protestants of all denominations have taught that Catholic doctrine deforms the authentic Gospel of Christ. If the Catholic Church were to join the W.C.C. now, a vast number of people in all the Churches, ignorant of the proper ecumenical distinctions, would be led into a confusion that could easily engender indifferentism or, which is equally bad, doctrinal syncretism. And nothing is further from the intention of the ecumenical movement!

On the other hand there are practical reasons against Catholic participation in the W.C.C. which, it seems to me, are internal to this Council itself. The W.C.C. has achieved unity among Christian Churches with very different traditions and basic outlooks. Many of these Churches, for various historical reasons, are afraid of the Roman Church and fear that friendship with Rome would endanger the freedom of their faith. If the Catholic Church were to come too close to the World Council, the now existing unity among the Churches might be endangered and some of the member Churches threaten to withdraw from the Council.

The W.C.C., moreover, seeks to be a Council for all Christian communions. It wants to remain basically open to the participation of the Catholic Church as well as of the many independent evangelical groups which have, until now, refused to join the ecumenical movement. On account of their present isolation, the friendship and collaboration of these independent groups is of greater importance for the total ecumenical picture than formal membership of the Catholic Church, involved as she is in the ecumenical dialogue in many other ways. If the Catholic Church came too close to the Council at this time, the hope of gaining the confidence of the evangelical Christians would be postponed indefinitely.

And, thirdly, one could mention that the participation of Rome in the W.C.C., with a representation in proportion to respective membership, would make the Catholic influence so strong that Protestants might no longer find themselves in the pronouncements and actions of the Council.

At the same time, not being a member of the W.C.C. does not exclude the Catholic Church from dialogue and cooperation in the ecumenical movement. At the Montreal Conference it was specifically stated that the ecumenical movement is larger than the W.C.C. This Council is only one manifestation of the movement for unity; there are others. In our day, there is no Church that can afford to be indifferent to dialogue with other Churches. Whether it is a question of interior renewal, of missionary work, of theological advance, or biblical studies, whether it is a matter of social doctrine or moral principles—no Church can do any of these things without engaging in dialogue with other Christians.

This was certainly acknowledged for the Catholic Church by Pope Paul VI in his speech at his coronation. The Pope declared that he "meant to pursue the dialogue, armed with charity and truth, and to advance as much as possible the work that has been undertaken."

Critical Remarks Examined

In this connection I wish to examine the critical remarks made by a speaker at the Montreal Conference. In a public lecture Dr. H. H. Harms has suggested that the present form of dialogue between the W.C.C. and private Catholic theologians does not really imply an ecumenical commitment on the part of the Catholic Church. He gave two reasons:

(1) The dialogue of unofficial theologians does not engage the Catholic Church, it remains a private endeavor, and if the Catholic Church does not approve of the results of the dialogue, she can easily repudiate them as well as the theologians involved in it. The Roman Church, moreover, does not share in the responsibility and common action which this dialogue should produce.

(2) The dialogue of uncommissioned theologians with the W.C.C. is not really a conversation on equal footing and therefore perhaps no dialogue at all. If the Catholic Church believes that she holds all the truth of the Gospel, then it would seem that in her eyes dialogue could be useful only to the others and not to her, and hence what looks like dialogue may be no two-way conversation at all.

These criticisms must be taken very seriously. In regard to the first point one must consider that the Catholic Church officially initiated dialogue when the Secretariat for Promoting Christian Unity was founded in Rome, when observers from the W.C.C. were invited to the Vatican Council and Catholic observers sent to World Council meetings. She actively engages in the ecumenical movement as a Church when she teaches her own members a new attitude toward other Christians. In fact, since the Roman Church teaches her members with authority, I believe that in this area of creating a new atmosphere of charity she is really more engaged in the ecumenical movement than other Churches, since these are often dependent in their teaching on the free cooperation of local groups. The Catholic Church is also deeply committed to the dialogue by taking into account, in her conciliar deliberations, the present ecumenical situation.

At the same time it is true that until now the Catholic Church has not sought ways to involve herself more concretely in the common action and common witness mediated by the W.C.C. It is here, I believe, that Dr. Harms' criticism has its foundation. Judging, however, from the rapid evolution of ecumenism in the Catholic Church in the last few years, it would not surprise me if, in the future, ways of collaborating with the W.C.C. were found, not through complete membership, but through more distant but nevertheless real participation in definite projects.

But what can be said about the second criticism? Is the Catholic Church, with her faith that she is the true Church of Christ, at all capable of

engaging in dialogue on equal footing? The answer depends on what we mean by "equal footing." If one means by this expression that both
partners start with the same notion of what the
Church is, then dialogue is not possible with
Rome; but then it is not possible either at the
W.C.C. among Protestants, Anglicans and Orthodox. In fact it would be quite unecumenical to
invite someone to an ecumenical dialogue on the
condition that he abandon an essential element
of his faith.

But if "equal footing" means what the Toronto
Declaration of the W.C.C. specifies about it, then
the ecclesiological problem is not prejudged and
dialogue is possible and, in fact, necessary. This
dialogue may not always be easy, because some
of the basic presuppositions of Protestants and
Catholics are different; but there is a real reciprocity in the sense that both Protestants and
Catholics acknowledge that all Christians belong
in some sense to the true Church of Christ and
that other Christian Churches bear in some sense
elements of this true Church. While the Catholic
is bound by his fidelity to the Word of God understood through the teaching of councils and
popes, he has learned and will learn much from
his Protestant partner that will make him purify
Catholic teaching and set it in a more evangelical
and balanced context. And while the Protestant
is bound by his central insight into the Gospel,
guided by his Church's understanding of the
Scriptures, he has learned and he will learn from
his Catholic partner much that was neglected, or
even had to be neglected, in the polemical days
of the Reformers.

Reciprocity in Dialogue

Reciprocity in the dialogue between Protestants and Catholics is real but subtle. It is not simple and spontaneous as in the dialogue between, for instance, Lutherans and Presbyterians. But the difference in certain basic doctrines does not in the slightest diminish our common conviction that we must make progress in understanding more deeply the teaching of Christ's Gospel, that we must conform the life of our Church, through liturgy and action, more profoundly to the Lord's plan of reconciliation, and that in this process, dialogue with others is indispensable today.

When I discussed this question at Montreal with the French Reformed theologian Jean Bosc and stressed that for a Catholic the other Churches are not Churches in the true sense, he pointed to the reciprocity in our relation by saying that the Reformed Christian does not regard the Catholic Church as a Church in the true sense either. He said "Vous jugez à partir de la plénitude, et nous à partir de l'authenticité"— "You make the judgment according to an ideal of fullness, and we according to an ideal of authenticity."

In terms of this reciprocity, Christians do not listen to one another enough.

13
Ecumenical Relations in Latin America

Jorge Mejia

THE ecumenical situation in Latin America is not easy to describe or appreciate. In the first place, contrary to what is believed in Europe and sometimes in North America, sociological and religious life in Latin America vary considerably from one country to another. In the second place, because inter-American communications are difficult, continental self-awareness is often colored by information that is incomplete and unreliable. All these limitations must be taken into account if one seeks a complete picture of our ecumenical situation.

By posing the question of ecumenical progress on our continent, we quietly assume that some real accomplishment has been achieved. However, it would be easier, and more exact, to speak about the beginnings of the Latin American ecumenical movement than about its accomplishments. In fact, after more than a century of indifferent and hostile co-existence, the Catholic and Protestant communities of Latin America are just beginning to recognize each other's existence. That is to say, they are just beginning to consider each other as Christians. This problem has deep roots, of which the most important is the character of Catholicism in Latin America as a sociologically established religion of the majority.

Protestantism in Latin America

Protestantism on the South American continent began as the religion of immigrants, and for a time it was no more than that. It was a personal factor in certain ethnic groups but it was not a social problem. That the English or German Protestant was not integrated into the Latin American social context, along with his own religion did not present a problem. Even when Protestants tended to increase in number, as they did in Argentina during the second half of the last century, their worship, often protected by the minority language, remained the religion of their own particular group.

With the second wave of immigration, shortly after the first, came members of the English Protestant Churches who were more interested in missionary work: Presbyterians, Methodists and others. And the situation was no longer the same. These new religious groups perceived keenly what was then the beginning of the Church's principal problem in Latin America: de-Christianization. A problem that continues today on a grand scale.

Latin America is not really a mission continent in the sense in which this word is used in official ecclesiastical language. Thanks in part to the admirable evangelical work of the Jesuits and other religious Orders during and after the conquest, the good news of salvation was proclaimed to almost the whole of the Indian population. At the same time it is also true—and we must not forget this—that the evangelization of the continent was interrupted almost violently by the suppression of the Jesuits at the end of the 18th century, and later by the various revolutions of independence with their resultant hostile liberalisms. Consequently, the missionary spirit of Protestantism found a fertile field in which to practice its apostolic activity.

In addition, it discovered a Catholicism in decadence. As evidenced throughout the world during the second half of the 19th century and the first years of the present century, Catholicism in Latin America was becoming a static religion. The Catholic life of faith tended to confine itself within the walls of church buildings. It was often reduced to practices of worship that were more superstitious than Christian. The public activity of Catholics when it existed was limited to the defense of the Church's rights in regard to social factors such as matrimony and education. Unconsciously, Catholics also defended their own position of sociological domination, which was continually being menaced despite the fact that certain provisions in our liberal constitutions attempted to prolong this dominance under more or less outdated forms.

For example, the Constitution of the Argentine Republic states that the President must be an apostolic Roman Catholic. This means, in practice, that he must have been baptized in the Catholic Church and nothing more. Certain Catholic groups wanted this "confessional" situation, inherited from the vice-royalty, to be revived, in a more conscientious manner. At one time such groups were of some importance, at least in certain countries. Today they are diminishing, although there is the danger that they may seek to embody their ideas in other forms, such as in the so-called "Catholic City."

This brief history is indispensable for the understanding of a complete picture of Catholic-Protestant relations in Latin America. While Catholicism has maintained its defensive posture, often leavened by a belligerence that is scarcely Christian, Protestantism, an essentially missionary movement, has maintained its aggressive spirit of enterprise.

Emergence of the "Sects"

The picture becomes more complex with the introduction of the "sects," insofar as they are distinct from the larger Protestant Churches which usually decline responsibility for such groups. Consider, for instance, the Pentecostals, who make up 80% of Chilean Protestants, the Jehovah's Witnesses and various other Evangelicals with their fundamentalist emphasis. This "third wave" of Protestants coincides with the development of working classes in our underdeveloped countries which were rapidly and haphazardly industrialized and thus deprived, at least partially, of their traditional rural populations. The problem of the poverty-stricken masses in Latin America and the growth of Protestantism are not as inseparable as they might seem to be at first glance.

Growth of Ecumenical Activity

The situation as it developed in Latin America, then, did not at all favor the evolution of an ecumenical movement. Ecumenical activity has appeared in the only place where it could under such circumstances—at the level of professional Scripture scholars, both Catholic and Protestant, trained at European or American universities. Accustomed to reading each other's books and journals, they tended to become acquainted with each other in the normal course of their work and through mutual involvement in the ecumenical movements of the Old World. The results were, and are bound to be, far-reaching, for professors' attitudes are reflected in the minds of their students who come to appreciate the reasons for these attitudes.

Already a new generation of priests and ministers, imbued with respect for each other as Christians, have been able, here and there, to undertake some common tasks such as urging the celebration of Easter and Christmas and advising matrimonial reunions. Moreover, and this is of great significance, important contacts now exist among the Catholic, the interdenominational and the Lutheran theological faculties of the Buenos Aires area, whose influence—at least in the case of Protestants—is felt throughout Latin America.

Influence of Vatican Council II

But it is the Vatican Council that has been able to break the ice definitively. And a deep crack has been opened in it. In this respect, the attitude of John XXIII was of utmost importance. His personal attitude in receiving bishops and ministers from other Churches, his creation of the Secretariat for the Promotion of Christian Unity and the subsequent invitation of non-Catholic observers to the Council—one of whom is a Latin American, the director of the Evangelical faculty of theology in Buenos Aires—are responsible for this thaw.

When everything is considered, one feels that the atmosphere is beginning to change. And this change affects both Catholics and Protestants. While Catholics are ceasing to be belligerent and defensive simply by trying to be Christian, Protestants, too, are modifying their attitudes. Signs of this rebirth are already in evidence throughout the South American continent. And this is true not only at the level of the faculties of theology, but among pastors of souls and the laity as well.

Cooperative Missionary Activity

Of course, there remain many important problems to be solved. Worthy of mention is the question of missionary activity. Protestants and Catholics should face this source of friction with profound mutual respect and in a spirit of Christian liberty. They should be conscious of the responsibility for the evangelization of this American continent, which is a problem too large and too urgent to be hindered by disputes. This is an ecumenical activity of the first order.

There are other problems. Catholics and Protestants in Latin America should be thinking seriously about the cooperative translation, printing and distribution of a popular edition of the Bible in order to avoid harmful competition. There is no reason why we should not take advantage of the exceptional Protestant experience in this field. The social needs of a continent in full fermentation of development are also fields ripe for ecumenical collaboration. Such cooperation is needed, not only to provide a common front against materialism, but also to seek, under the sign of Christianity, the amelioration of conditions that are, at times, subhuman in Latin America. This cannot be accomplished unless there is prior testimony of mutual charity.

On our continent, as in other parts of the world, Christian unity presents itself to Catholics and Protestants alike as a communal and personal mandate of the Lord whom we all wish to serve. To be unfaithful to this call is to be unfaithful to the Lord in whom we have all been baptized.

14

Ecumenism in Africa—Reflections of a Bishop

Bishop J. Blomjous

IT is not easy to make general remarks about the ecumenical situation on the African continent, since conditions vary from country to country and each part has its own particular history. It is nonetheless possible to spell out certain common factors which, in varying proportions, influence the mutual relation of the Christian Churches in Africa.

Common Factors in African Ecumenism

Africa is a continent of mission territories or, as many prefer to put it today, of young Churches. While the missionary movement in the Protestant world was the cradle of the ecumenical movement and the Edinburgh Conference of 1910 is regarded by many as the starting point of an organized ecumenical effort, the missionaries themselves were, in the past, not particularly interested in ecumenism. They were overwhelmed by the amount of work at the local station and hence often unwilling to spare the time for ecumenical conversations.

In recent years, however, the ecumenical movement has made rapid progress among the young Churches. There are several reasons for this. These young Churches do not feel the weight of history. Catholic bishops and Christian leaders in general are today often African-born, conscious of their vocation as Africans, and they react against Christian divisions as an importation from European culture. They do not wish to be burdened with the conflicts of long ago; what counts for them is the present. Once ecumenical conversations begin, these men have fewer inhibitions, they are held back by fewer prejudices. For this reason we find that in Africa, in contradistinction to the European and, perhaps, the American scene, the ecumenical movement is sponsored first of all by the hierarchy. It is not so much a movement from below as from above. In many countries it was the Episcopal Conference that appointed specialists to study ecumenical problems and arranged for contacts and meetings of various kinds with other Christian Churches.

What are some of the common factors that influence the African ecumenical movement in a positive way?

1. *The Missionary Factor.* In the past the missionary character of the African Churches was a handicap for the growth of an ecumenical spirit. The mission of one Church tended to look upon other missions as competitive move-

ments; and since they all regarded the missionary movement as a conquest of souls, there were occasions when they worked against one another and did not avoid open conflict. This age is now basically gone. In the first place, Christians have come to understand the missionary drive of the Church in different terms, not as a conquest of souls, but, rather, as a witness and service offered to human society. In the second place, Christians of the Catholic Church and other Christian communions have come to realize that they face together a non-Christian world of vast proportions. Understanding the mission of the Church in such terms has helped, as we shall see below, the advance of the ecumenical movement.

2. *The non-Western Factor.* The division of the Churches is regarded by Africans as an importation from the European nations, and they begin to react as strongly against it as they do against other harmful imported goods. Especially, in the newly created countries do Christians of all communions want to collaborate. In some cases, the national unity of the new State depends on the cooperation and friendship among the various Christian groups, and it is not surprising that this social pressure makes Christians impatient with the divisions of the past.

3. *The Factor of Underdevelopment.* The African continent is mainly composed of underdeveloped countries or, to use a more polite expression, of countries of rapid social and economic change. For this reason the social services which the Churches offer to society are of the greatest importance. In the past this provided occasion for strife and argument. For some time

now, the spirit of competition has been replaced
by the willingness to cooperate, and since these
social services have acquired great importance,
even in government planning, there have been
many occasions for the Churches to meet and
discuss their common social aims. In several
countries, Christians of all Churches stand together on questions regarding schools and hospi-
tals, and a single spokesman represents their
interests before the national government.

4. *The African Factor.* While it is difficult to
generalize about the particular trends of a people, especially when this people is spread over a
whole continent, it may be said that the highest
value in the life of the ordinary African is good
human relations. Much of his behavior and many
of his reactions are determined by the desire to
establish friendship with his neighbor. In the
past this effort to build human relations was
confined to his own community and generated
an enormous attachment to family, tribe and
group, and for that reason impeded the ecumenical movement. Africans did not easily leave their
community to find friendship with outsiders. But
today, thanks to the new nationalism, this intention of building good human relations is a strong
factor in favor of ecumenism.

5. *A Factor of Ambiguity.* Christians of the
young African Churches have little interest in
doctrinal matters. What counts for them is the
Christian life and the pastoral problems of the
community. Africans often are not interested in
the fine points of doctrine over which the
Churches have fought in Europe for many centuries. This attention to practical and immedi-

ate matters is of great advantage for the ecumenical movement, but it also has its dangers. It can be a stimulus for greater collaboration, but it can also present a new obstacle. Syncretism in any form will always harm the spread of the Gospel and hinder the movement for Christian unity.

6. *The Colonial Factor.* African Christians, more than their Asian brethren, are strongly marked by the culture of their former colonial lords. The Francophone Churches, *i.e.*, the Churches in which the clergy received their education in French, reflect the strength and, perhaps, some of the weakness characteristic of French Christianity, and the Anglophone Churches, where the clergy has been educated in English, reflect what is most characteristic of British and/or Irish Christianity. For this reason the ecumenical movement in these respective areas reproduce, to some extent, the forms and methods of ecumenism in the French and in the English-speaking world.

After this rapid survey of the main factors influencing the present situation of ecumenism in Africa, I wish to present some personal reflections on the nature and role of ecumenism in the future development of the African Church. I would like to point out from the beginning that these personal reflections were born in the atmosphere of the African apostolate, which obliges us constantly to confront the message of the Gospel with the hard facts of reality and to rethink the meaning of the Church's mission. The fundamental problem in our reflection on the Church's mission—and on ecumenism, which belongs to that mission—lies in the theological meaning of the fact of religious pluralism.

Religious Pluralism—Part of God's Plan?

We used to think that the Church was sent into the world to gain the adherence of all men to Christ, and that her missionary effort was destined to convert all men to live as brothers in a single Church. While we realized that this aim was not to be achieved in our lifetime, we did feel that through our missionary effort we hastened the coming of this happy day. Today, however, we are faced with the realization that pluralism, and specifically religious pluralism, is established in most parts of the world, and that the forces of history will eventually make it a universal phenomenon.

Sober statistics tell us that Christians represent a smaller percentage of the world population in every decade. With the shrinking globe, moreover, we can no longer speak of any uniformly Christian area or country, in the sense that the Christian Church and national culture are coextensive. These patterns belong to the past. It seems that religious pluralism is part of God's plan. Can we still assert that the Lord has sent his Church into the world to gather all men in the unity of faith? We are forced to ask ourselves the serious question: what is the theological meaning of religious pluralism? What is God attempting to tell us through the multiplicity of religions?

There is a second equally uncomfortable question: it deals with the divisions of Christians into separate communities. As Catholics we believe that Christ meant all the baptized to live in a single Church founded upon the Twelve with Peter, and in the past we used to imagine, or accept as an ideal, that the Church's missionary drive may become so strong among non-Catholic Christians that one day they will all come back to us. For practical reasons, if not for deeper theological ones, this dream has come to an end.

Christian pluralism is not a passing phenomenon, not a temporary illness to be healed by an avalanche of conversions or a series of successful mergers. In a sinful world there will always be, against the will of God, tensions and strife. The movements for unity may be blessed with happy fruits, but after each union new trouble may provoke other divisions; this is the situation of our fallen race. Christians are certainly destined to seek the unity which is Christ's will for his people, and, as Catholics, we believe that the unity of faith, liturgy and ecclesiastical communion is indefectibly present in the Catholic Church; and yet it appears that the division of Christians will be with us until the end of time. We must rather ask the question: what is God trying to tell us through these divisions?

Missionary Task of Church Today

As we read the Scriptures to find answers to our questions we notice that in the New Testament Christians are compared to a leaven destined to leaven the whole dough, and to a light meant to illumine the entire world. If Christians are called "the little flock," one may well wonder whether the Church is not meant to remain in the diaspora situation in which she lived in New

Testament times. There is no assurance in the Scriptures that the Gospel which is to be preached in all parts of the world will actually bring the Christian faith to all men and make them members of the Christian Church. Is not, rather, the Church meant to be a minority in the human family?

If this is so, then the missionary task of the Church must be understood in a deeper fashion. It cannot be equated with the conquest of souls. Its aim is not defined by the maximum of unbelievers to be brought to the Christian faith. If the Church is "light" and "leaven" in society, then her mission is a work of *witness and service* offered to the human community, and it is up to the inscrutable wisdom of God whether this effort will result in conversions to the faith or more especially in the transformation of the social climate.

The Church is not destined simply to save men for heaven but also to humanize man's social life, to inspire a sense of personal responsibility in all men, and to foster a social order that sins less flagrantly against divine justice. In other words, the mission of the Church is to bring the peoples of the world into the redemptive plan of God, to lead them to play an active part in the fulfillment of this plan for humanity, but we have no way of knowing whether this plan, at this particular moment of history, foresees their conversion to the Christian faith.

Regarding the Church's mission not as a conquest of souls or territories, but as a humble witness and service offered to society, gives us a new confidence and keeps us from discourage-

ment when we do not see the success of our work.
The Spirit rules the Church as he wills, and we
cannot foresee how God will make use of our
efforts in the advance of the kingdom. This attitude will overcome the unhappy competition
between the Churches, which has characterized
the mission fields in the past. We leave perfect
liberty to other Christians and do not rush things
according to our own measure of understanding.

Theological Meaning of Disunity

This leads us to the second question we have
posed. What is the theological significance of
Christian disunity? What does God try to teach
us through the fact of our division? Since divisions among Christians, though against the will
of God, are the permanent situation into which
the Church is set, ecumenism cannot be regarded
as a temporary remedy or a modern fashion soon
to be out of date but as a permanent and essential function of the Church's life. Speaking to us
through the fact of Christian disunity, God pre-
vents us from keeping our eyes fixed on the fullness of gifts received by the Catholic Church and
saves us from regarding our divisions as a temporary phenomenon capable of being rectified
through individual conversions. Ecumenism, or
the quest for unity engaging the Catholic Church
and other Christian communions, is a permanent
and essential function of the Church.

What does this "unitive function" of the
Church aim at? It seeks to bring together all
the Christian Churches or communions in the
unity which is God's will for his people and
which, according to the Catholic faith, will al-

ways be in continuity with the Church of Peter. But what are the means, or some of the means, by which we try to bring all the Christian Churches and communions into greater obedience to the Lord? How do we practice ecumenism?

Practical Ecumenism

(a) Ecumenism means that we must help all Christians, Catholics and others, to live their Christianity more faithfully. This is not a betrayal of the unicity of the Catholic Church, but on the contrary a realistic appraisal of the function of this Church in an inevitably pluralistic Christendom. I believe that all the help and friendship we give to other Christians, and this applies especially to the African situation, is a contribution to the ecumenical movement and prepares the unity toward which the Lord is moving us. To become more Christian is surely the will of God for all who believe and are baptized, and by helping Christians in and outside her borders in this way, the Catholic Church helps them to enter more fully into God's plan for them.

(b) Ecumenism means that we listen to God speaking to us through other Christians. The existence of separated Churches accuses the one Church of the Lord of infidelity, for if she had been more faithful to the Gospel, God would not have permitted the division of his people. Our division is a constant call to the conversion of the heart. But we must also listen to others as partners in a dialogue. They have left the unity of the Church because of an emphasis, excessive in our eyes, on a particular Christian truth and hence this very truth may be alive among them in a specially developed form. We must learn from others in whatever way possible, knowing that whatever is wise and holy comes from God.

(c) Ecumenism means seeking ever greater areas of collaboration. Catholic bishops have long urged for collaboration in the temporal order with other Christians and indeed with all men of good will; but even beyond the purely temporal order, there are areas involving religion itself where collaboration is possible and even imperative. This raises a difficult question, for we cannot minimize the evil of indifferentism nor the harm done by scandal, but it is a question that we cannot avoid in Africa. What is a scandal in Europe or America may not be a scandal on the African continent. I wish to give two examples of specifically religious areas where collaboration should be sought.

First, there should be common Christian influence on the Islamic cultures. This common effort will not consist in converting Mohammedans to the Christian faith, but, more realistically, in helping Islam to become an open religion, to detach itself from past links with national governments and to live in a pluralistic society in which all religions are able to make their special contribution to the common good. And secondly, there should be a common Christian confrontation with the modern industrialized world. Again, this common effort will not aim at converting men to the Christian faith, it will, rather, attempt to convey a deeper understanding of what our earthly existence means: labor, industry and the unification and socialization that move in upon us. Marxists are able to prepare their followers ideologically for the understanding of the present world so that they remain sane and productive under the strain of modern life; while the Gospel contains a superior key to the meaning of our daily work, we are on the whole unable to communicate it to society. Here cooperation is imperative.

15
The Changing "Y"

Paul Broadhurst

BETWEEN July 8 and 12, 1962, the World YWCA and the World Alliance of YMCAs held a "Joint Consultation on Ecumenical Policy and Practice for Lay Christian Movements" at St. Cerque in Switzerland. The significance of this meeting can, perhaps, best be appreciated in the light of the development of these movements through their hundred-year history.

Foundation and Growth of YMCA

The YMCA was founded in 1844 in London, England, by a group of young men who believed that the young men of their day would benefit from an organization which worked for their spiritual betterment in a spirit of Christian fellowship. All young men who gave evidence of conversion to God were welcome to share in the services which the Y provided and in the labor of providing them for others. The activities characteristic of the organization in its beginnings were prayer meetings and Bible classes. Through these activities it tried to influence young people to lead religious lives. It wasn't long, however, before its service to others was broadened to include the field of social action. By 1851, the YMCA had come to North America. In its first American foundation, in Boston, particular emphasis was laid upon the Association as a social center. It is in Boston, too, that we see appear the plan of restricting full membership with voting and office-holding rights to those who were members in good standing of an Evangelical (Protestant) Church.

By 1855, the Associations had spread to many lands, and that year marked the first meeting of representatives from YMCAs throughout the world. At this convention was adopted the "Paris Basis," a statement of purpose and a criterion for membership: "The Young Men's Christian Associations seek to unite those young men who, regarding Jesus Christ as their God and Savior according to the Holy Scriptures, desire to be his disciples in their doctrine and in their life, and to associate their efforts for the extension of his kingdom among young men." Seen in the context of the theological implications it would have had for Catholics of that time, the "Paris Basis" established clearly, though perhaps unintentionally, that the Y was an almost exclusively Protestant association. The later practice of limiting full membership to Protestants together with the Evangelical orientation of its religious and spiritual service left no doubt of this.

As the number of Associations increased more emphasis was placed, particularly in America, on a broadened area of service to include the social, intellectual and physical, as well as the spiritual, improvement of young men. This expanding interest, destined eventually to become world-wide, was based upon the idea that a Christian must seek the development of all his powers as a human being and must use all of them in the service of his God. Yet the evangelical character of the Associations remained strong in America. The Portland convention of North American Associations in 1869 decided to accept for all American Associations the same basis for full membership which had been adopted in the pioneer Association of Boston. Only members of Evangelical Churches should vote or hold office in the Associations: "We hold those Churches to be Evangelical which maintaining the Holy Scriptures to be the only infallible rule in faith and practice, do believe in the Lord Jesus Christ (the only begotten Son of the Father, King of Kings, and Lord of Lords, in whom dwelleth the fullness of the Godhead bodily, and who was made sin for us though knowing no sin, bearing our sins in his own body on the tree) as the only name under heaven given among men whereby we must be saved from everlasting punishment." By 1870, then, the North American YMCAs though bearing no official relationship to any one Protestant Church, were associations of Protestant Christian inspiration, working for the physical, intellectual, social and spiritual welfare of young men.

Foundation and Growth of YWCA

The growth of the YWCA parallels very closely that of the YMCA. It had its beginnings in 1855,

in England. In that year were founded two
groups of young women, one a prayer union with
purely spiritual aims, the other an institution of
social service providing homes for young business
women. In 1887 the two groups united in the
YWCA to seek the all-round welfare of Christian
young women. The first constitution of the World
YWCA adopted in 1898 accepted as its basis a
strongly Evangelical statement intended for a
group whose membership was almost entirely
"limited to young women who are members in
good standing of an Evangelical Church."

The growth of the Associations was phenome-
nal. As they spread throughout the world, it became inevitable that they be introduced into
countries where Protestant Christianity was not
the predominant religion. In these countries,
where membership would have to be largely Orthodox or Roman Catholic, the evangelical basis
of full membership had to be de-emphasized. The
presence of delegates from such Associations at
world conventions began to raise problems. Thus,
for example, from the time of the Stockholm Conference of 1914 the YWCA was faced with the
dilemma of delegates who could not ask their
members to make a personal commitment to a
doctrinal position which did not adequately en-
compass their own religion. The YMCA, of
course, met with the same difficulties. It was far
from easy for organizations which had been
originally founded on the basis of Evangelical
Christianity and whose initial purpose was to
propagate this religion among the young, to en-
visage a resolution of the situation. It is true that
their purpose was no longer solely religious,

but their vision of Christianity was still the motivating force behind their services to the young. The Associations were to grapple with this problem for many years to come.

Position of Catholic Church

In the meantime, the Catholic Church found it necessary to take a position regarding membership of Catholics in the Ys. A directive issued from Rome, November 5, 1920, informed Catholic bishops of its appraisal of the YMCA and YWCA. These groups are not, the directive pointed out, for Catholic participation. The Evangelical basis of the Ys made such a statement inevitable. The official Catholic evaluation of the Associations insofar as Catholic membership is concerned remains the same to our own day. In 1954, a reiteration of the original appraisal came from the Congregation of the Holy Office in Rome. The bishops of some local Catholic dioceses have since seen fit to restate this prohibition for their own people. The danger they saw for Catholics was indifferentism to religion. How can a Catholic take part in an organization which, both in theory and in practice, seems to deny some aspects of his Catholic faith? If a Catholic joins a YMCA or YWCA with its heavily Protestant orientation, is he not by that very fact compromising his own faith, and will he not feel, as time passes, that it really doesn't matter to what Church he belongs, be it Catholic or Protestant? The problem needed no delineation; its lines were, for the Catholic, clearly drawn. A bishop, except in unusual circumstances, could adopt no other official position.

The Y's New Constitution

However, the long searching within the Ys with regard to their Evangelical basis and their non-Protestant members was not to be fruitless. Gradually through the 1920s and 1930s the Y was able to work out agreements with several Orthodox Churches, thus involving itself more deeply with non-Protestant traditions. In 1947, the World's Committee of the YMCA recommended "that the World's Committee facilitate the exchange of experience among leaders of the YMCA in Roman Catholic communities, and urge that ways be discovered whereby all members may participate fully in the privileges and responsibilities of the Association." The World's Committee of 1953 issued a directive regarding national constitutions, something it rarely does: "The Constitutions of National Alliances should be consistent with the established interconfessional policy and practice of the World's Committee as set out in the various relevant decisions taken by it in recent years. They should, therefore, give expression to the principle that members of the YMCA seek to live and achieve the purposes of the Movement in accordance with the teachings and spirit of the Church to which they belong, whilst giving full respect to the religious convictions of other members."

Long before these last two events, the YMCAs of the United States and Canada, at their 1931 convention, replaced the Portland Basis of 1869 with a new statement in which the YMCA was described as "a world-wide fellowship of men and boys united by a common loyalty to Jesus Christ for the purpose of developing Christian personality and building a Christian society."

In 1955 the YWCA held a World Council meeting near London, England. The desire to be open to all Christians resulted in constitutional changes. Thus, for example, the YWCA adopted as the basis for its new constitution: "Faith in God the Father Almighty and in Jesus Christ his only Son our Lord and Savior and in the Holy Spirit."

Describing the functions of the YWCA the new constitution continued: "It brings women and girls of different Christian traditions into a world-wide fellowship through which they may grow as Christians, participating in the life and worship of their Church and expressing their faith by word and deed. It includes within its fellowship all women and girls who desire to participate in its program." The group studying "Our Christian Fellowship" at the 1955 Council meeting made the following suggestions to National Associations: "That they recognize their responsibility to help members to deepen their personal belief within their own Church and to grow in the knowledge and understanding of different Christian traditions. That they keep constantly before them their task in helping non-church-going members to find their place in the fellowship of a Church." Gone is the Protestant basis of membership and the exclusively Evangelical inspiration of activity.

Having passed through this long and at times painful evolution, the Ys now seek to bring together lay people from all the different Christian confessions — Orthodox, Roman Catholic and

Protestant — in a fellowship in which they can express their Christian faith in action for the benefit of their communities. The member is indeed expected to strengthen his Christian life through working for others in the Y, but the nourishing of this life through Word and Sacraments is to take place within his own Church. Recent years have, then, witnessed a significant evolution in the purposes and ideal of the YMCA and YWCA.

Ecumenical Policy

It is with this background that the World YWCA and the World Alliance of YMCAs held their "Joint Consultation on Ecumenical Policy and Practice for Lay Christian Movements" at St. Cergue, Switzerland. Here some sixty persons, YMCA and YWCA representatives together with consultants, fraternal delegates— Orthodox, Protestant and Roman Catholic— joined informally in prayer, Bible study and discussion on questions of ecumenical policy. Participation in the program by a Greek Orthodox bishop, two Dominican priests, Protestant clergymen as well as by laymen of these Churches marked significantly the progress which the ecumenical movement within the Ys had made in recent years.

Even in the past, ecumenical interest has been no stranger among members of these organizations. Their intense Christian zeal had led them to an appreciation of the scandal of divided Christendom. Their generosity and world vision have in fact supplied the leadership of the great Protestant ecumenical organizations. So true is

this that at the founding convention of the
World Council of Churches in Amsterdam, 1948,
the large majority of those assembled on the
platform owed their ecumenical inspiration to
some connection with the YMCA or YWCA.
And yet, because of their original Protestant
inspiration, the ecumenical interest and activity
of Y members had confined itself to the Protestant Churches.

One of the most striking aspects of the 1962
Consultation was the repeatedly expressed awareness of the wider horizons which ecumenism must
have for them. This was undoubtedly an effect of
the World Council of Churches on the Christian
conscience. Careful thought was given to what it
means to individuals to belong to an Association
that brings together members from different confessions and what it must mean to the Association to have that kind of membership. In the
words of Dr. Paul M. Limbert, General Secretary
of the World Alliance of YMCAs: "We want
leaders of the Churches to understand better
what our two movements are, and to advise us
of some of the factors that should determine our
policy and practice if we mean to take the
Churches — *all* the Churches — very seriously."
Over and over again was stressed the importance
of realizing that since the Ys seek the participation of all Christians in their work, they must be
extremely careful to avoid anything which might
bring harm to the conscience of any member. The
Christian faith of the members must always remain the motive force behind all their work, but
in the traditional prayer and Bible study in which
the members participate, some way must be

found to avert any shadow of bias. This, of course, is a difficult problem and was seen as such, yet solutions can be reached. Thus, for example, in a working paper on this problem, the YWCA of Canada suggests to its member Associations that the prayer at its meetings not take the form of worship in any official sense, but that it be, rather, in the form of family prayer in which all can join without hesitation. It suggests too that Bible study, though it be very important for Y members — precisely because they are Christian—need not be done in groups, but can be done just as well privately. Thus the specifically religious aspects of the Association meetings can remain for each member in the context of his or her own religious tradition.

The YMCA and YWCA, in their first one hundred years, have indeed undergone a quiet evolution. From a beginning deeply imbedded in the traditions of Evangelical Protestantism they have moved to a position of openness to all Christians, openness to the extent of wanting the leaders of all communions to help them develop a program in which all Christians can take part with no harm done to conscience.

Meaning of Change for Catholics

Does this have any meaning for members of the Catholic Church? Perhaps we should first realize that development has also taken place in recent years among Catholics—a striking growth in the realization of what it means to be a Christian. Many examples of this could be cited. In his two recent encyclicals, Pope John XXIII called to the attention of Catholics that their

mission as Christians is to the world, that they
must bring their Christian influence to bear on a
world that is far from Christian, that the common good and welfare of their fellow men is of
deepest concern. Again, while coming to a new
awareness of the pain that separation must bring
to all Christians, Catholics have been urged to
appreciate the fact that all separated Christians,
washed in the life-giving and saving waters of
Christ's baptism, possessing his Holy Spirit, are
in union with his Mystical Body. Suspicion, rival-
ry and hate ill-become sons of the Father in
Christ. Further, this has led to the possibility of
Christians of different Churches praying together, not in official worship—this is one of the
prices we must pay for our separation—but in the
fellowship of our common heritage as Christians.

Can we not foresee, then, perhaps even in the
near future, the possibility of a change in the
official Catholic evaluation of the YMCA and
YWCA? Would it be overly sanguine to envision
Christians, including Catholics, nourished in the
traditions and worship of their own Churches,
praying together for inspiration and guidance in
their work, going out in Christian fellowship to
a world which knows not Christ, to work for the
spiritual, intellectual, social and physical betterment of all men?

One must, of course, be realistic in dealing with
a matter such as this. There are difficulties in the
way. For example, it is simply a fact that the
enunciation of policy on the highest level of organizations such as the YMCA and YWCA is not
identical with the implementation of such policy
on the national and local levels. Because the

basic unit of the Ys is the local Association, fed-
erated in national organizations and related
through them to the world alliance, the extent
to which such policy is actually adopted in any
given local Association will depend almost entirely on the members of that Association. Thus
we find today some Associations which are fully
aware of the latest developments of policy in the
world groups and anxious to implement such
policy as soon as possible. On the other hand we
also find local Associations which are hardly
aware of or concerned with such changes of
policy, still bearing a heavily Evangelical orientation. Some of these are still anti-Catholic in
tone and distribute literature misrepresenting the
Catholic Church.

At the same time we must realize that we also
find two divergent attitudes among Catholics,
one, of longstanding, tending to hostility, and
the other, of rather recent origin, tending to cooperation. Even if, on the part of the Y in a
certain area, participation was possible, yet the
Catholic community of that area would have to
undergo an evolution so that the people become
conscious of the new trends in the Church and
appreciate the meaning of the venture in which
they are about to engage.

In some cities the Ys spend most of their effort
in helping young people to grow up as responsible
citizens by providing educational and recrea-
tional facilities. The aim of the Associations in
these areas is simply to raise the moral tone of
the community, to prevent juvenile delinquency,
and encourage young people to respond to what
is best in them. In such a climate the collabora-

tion would not pose the religious problems mentioned above.

It becomes apparent that it is quite impossible today to generalize on the relation of Catholics and Protestants and, more especially, on the relation of Catholics to the Ys. Since movements of renewal and re-evaluation are presently operative in all the Churches, this relation depends on the extent to which the ecumenical evolution has affected the local situation. Hence the need of personal contacts and information through dialogue! Diocese will differ from diocese in this matter, and because the bishop bears ultimate responsibility for his diocese, he has the authority to direct all such developments in the Church under his care.

Taking all these factors into consideration, it could be said that the development of approved Catholic participation in the YMCA and YWCA, were it to come, would be (for the communities where it could be realized) a great step in the direction of the cooperation of Christians in working for the welfare of their fellow men and a new accomplishment in Christian understanding.

Part IV

ECUMENICAL
DIALOGUE

16

Attitudes Toward
the Reformation

Richard M. Saunders

THE Reformation may be looked at in three
ways: as a series of events in time, as a
period of history and as an attitude of mind
which is a continuing thing. We have now
reached a point where there is general agreement
among Catholic, Protestant and rationalist historians as to the basic factual narrative. On the
scholarly level this is evidenced in the work of
men like Hughes, Bainton and Hulme. More
important, in the standard college textbook accounts, such as those of Carlton J. Hayes, Fer-
guson and Brunn, and R. R. Palmer, we encounter the same basic agreement, at least as far
as the factual narrative is concerned.

Interpretation, on the other hand, involving as
it does a continuing attitude of mind, a selection
and weighing of the facts, can result in a very
different over-all picture. What is significant is
that over the past fifty years Catholic and Protestant accounts have become so similar even in

matters of interpretation. Especially in this century, historians on both sides have been increasingly willing to study sympathetically the attitudes, the ideas and the values as well as the events of the Reformation. Extremes and differences still exist, but as scholarship progresses the extent of unanimity has become truly remarkable.

To understand the Reformation as a continuing thing, we must trace the various historical attitudes that have been taken throughout the centuries. In the beginning the original movement was a revolution, or more correctly, a civil war with all the violence and bitterness of such events. It was exacerbated by what we today would call the ideological character of the struggle. The Reformation was a spiritual division, or so it seemed to the parties that were involved then and for so long.

For historiography the result was an intense historical investigation for the purpose of providing justification for each side. In other words, the historiography of the Reformation turned out to be for a very long time a running polemic, a battle of books. It was part of the cold-hot war of the 16th century. Even so, despite the polemical tone and atmosphere, men as irreligious as Jules Michelet or as religious as Lord Acton or as professionally historical in their viewpoint as Leopold von Ranke have all remarked upon the benefit to historical research that has been derived even from controversies such as that between Protestant and Catholic.

The 18th-Century Humanists

By the 18th century the struggle had subsided

into a stalemate with both sides more or less
withdrawing into themselves. In the scholarly
world at that time a deep reaction developed
against religious strife. There was a strong desire
to bring an end to this kind of conflict and to
avoid it in the future. The Deists, the Philosophers and the *Illuminati* of the 18th-century
Enlightenment strove to end what they considered irrational strife and to bring rational peace
among rational men. Stressing education and
swept up in a wave of optimism, these secular
humanists believed in man's capacity to control
his own destiny, to control nature and to control
society: such convictions openly disclaimed all
kinds of organized orthodox religious belief.

Certain historical writers of the Enlightenment
saw the Reformation as a welcome loosening of
authority and tradition, a step toward that freedom of thought which they were advising so
strongly and putting so much hope upon, a prerequisite, in other words, for the new rational
society. For others, it was a series of examples of
irrational strife, the sort of thing that had to be
quelled and eliminated from the new enlightened
society. In Voltaire's mind, for example, the St.
Bartholomew's Day massacre and Cromwell's
treatment of the Irish belonged in the same category as examples of the irrationality of religious
struggle. For Voltaire, the Quakers were an ideal
because while their religious ideas were simply
absurd, their peaceful, reasonable conduct was
magnificent.

The 18th century thereby introduced, or
rather re-emphasized, the third strand in the Re-

formation struggle—the humanist strand. The
Reformation was never a two-sided quarrel. One
of the chief Protestant charges was that the Old
Church had surrendered too much to Renaissance Humanism, that is, to non-Christian or
classical or pagan culture and that therefore it
was not adequately fulfilling its proper function
of spiritual leadership. The Catholic rebuttal was
that Protestant individualism and sectarianism
would certainly prove to be the logical road toward a decline in Christian faith and loyalty and
would end in producing a worldly lot of humanistic beliefs in society.

Both Protestants and Catholics recognized the
Christian spiritual element in the struggle as well
as the secular humanistic divergencies from it.
The possible victory of the last, the secular
humanists, was certainly considered to be an un-
desirable result by both Catholics and Protestants. But, by the 18th century, the secular
humanist trend, the third party, was armed with
a new optimism of Cartesian hope and conviction. These secular humanists were also aided by
the reaction to religious strife and motivated by
the vision of a human, earthly, perfectible society.

Condorcet, "the perfect *philosophe*," relegated
the Reformation to a stage in the development
toward the perfect society, a stage which is more
to be identified with the irrational past than with
the rational future of man. This point of view
became deeply entrenched in historical writing
and is commonly found in textbooks well into
the 20th century. Not only religious conflict and
religious strife but even religious life itself was

de-emphasized as something passing away just as the irrational past was considered to be giving way to the new rational society. This liberal-rationalist view in historiography came to downgrade the religious factor in all historical development even apart from the Reformation, Such an attitude retained the ascendancy for a century or more.

19th-Century Romanticism

Meanwhile, the 19th century brought new factors into the picture and so into historical interpretation. The first of these was Romanticism. The Romantics were, among other things, deeply concerned with the individuality of persons, places, periods and times of past history. In this sense, Leopold von Ranke is the most outstanding example of a Romantic historian. Ranke was interested in discovering uniqueness, not universality. Ranke insisted that we must get back to the real thing. We must find out what really happened, not what we think happened but what really happened.

Ranke's second cardinal principle was that every historical period was in direct relation to God. This meant that every period of history is worthy of study for its own sake and no historical period is to be judged or sacrificed for the truth of any future whatsoever. Each period is to be understood in the light of its own standards, ideas and circumstances. Why? Because all peoples, all ages, all historical periods are of equal value in the eyes of God. For von Ranke, Providence rules history and all that an historian can do is to lift the veil a bit, look at the mystery and worship. That kind of emphasis presents a problem to many modern historians because so many of them are confined to a secularized point of view and have become what are called "historicists."

Von Ranke's insistence on knowing history as it really was for the sake of knowing the truth, when applied to the Reformation played a large role in closing the gap of understanding and in achieving the growing agreement on the factual narrative concerning the Reformation. To try to get at the facts for the sake of historical truth has proven a most valuable and fruitful principle for arriving at real knowledge about the Reformation. In the long run it has proven a healing principle in religion.

Dialectical Materialism

But there is a second aspect of 19th-century thinking which has had a profound effect upon historiography, namely the belief in dialectical materialism. This historical interpretation is now being taught to one-third, and perhaps even more, of the population of the world. Under Marx and Engels materialism took on a new form. They explained that instead of ideas being predominant in the development of history, it was rather a deterministic, dialectical, materialistic process in which class struggle was the basic dynamic of the process. This is the process which will end finally in a perfect society where government will wither away and men will live rationally ever after.

Marx was himself a 19th-century romantic in that he based his Utopian dream on the eventual arrival of a perfect society, and on his excitement over the miseries of the working class. He combined this genuine sympathy with a Rousseauan belief in the goodness of man. He was convinced that man can know and utilize the determining laws of nature. For Marx, however, all cultural, ideological, spiritual and religious factors are epiphenomena, functions, reflections of material conditions, that is, without a life or independence of their own.

Men possessing such a materialistic outlook would have a radically different historical interpretation of the Reformation. Facts that looked perfectly real to other historians did not look real at all to Marxist historians. Engels saw the Reformation as a social revolutionary development motivated by the shifting interests of new economic classes aiming to seize control of the means of production and thus of society. Any idea of real spiritual struggle being involved in the Reformation was completely scuttled. At best, religion was held to be hallucination, illusion, phantom, and at worst was seen as a calculated instrument of class war. It was certainly never seen as a fundamental reality in the historical situation. Today, at the University of Jena, for example, of the twenty-one graduate courses offered in the department of History, only one pertains even remotely to the Reformation, and it is entitled "The Peasants' Revolt, An Example of Proletarian Struggle."

It should be a matter of profound concern to historians and especially to Christian historians that such an interpretation should be so widespread and increasingly influential. Not that a

Christian historian denies economic influences and interests or even their connection with religious strife. What does concern such historians is the failure on the part of the Marxist historians to see any reality whatsoever to spiritual life. To the Christian historian this is an unrealistic recording of human experiences because it denies spirituality, particularly the Christian concept of spiritual life lived in a divinely governed world within providential history. It denies to that concept any true or essential validity.

The Marxist interpretation states that so far as the Reformation is concerned, Catholics and Protestants were not really and could not have been really quarreling about real spiritual values or beliefs. It states that both sides were unwittingly involved in the dialectical process, that is, that they believed themselves to be fighting about spiritual things while they were actually swept away by the materialistic, deterministic evolution of human society.

Mid-20th-Century Historical Research

In this mid-20th century, the differences over which Catholic and Protestant fought in the Reformation and continued to fight over for so long seem rather less divisive, rather less important to the descendants of those who fought than those ideas and views which divide them both from either the secular humanist or the dialectical materialist. The growing cooperation and agreement on Reformation research by Christian scholars is based to a great extent on the growing realization—on the part of those who hold history to be under the governance of God's authority and who see the need of seeing history in the light of spiritual verities—that they really have a great deal in common.

Even in a family quarrel like the Reformation —and it is a family quarrel—they have far more in common with each other than they have with those who see history only as a determined process of non-divine forces. Indeed, as Reformation studies are more and more pursued in the light of history as it really was, it is revealed that the two religious parties to the quarrel, like family foes, have always had more in common than they could ever see in the midst of a conflict that has unfortunately gone on far too long.

17

The Changing Image of Luther

F. M. Quealey

IN recent years Catholic historians have been seriously re-evaluating Martin Luther both as an historical figure and as a symbol. The violence and religious strife that accompanied the Reformation precluded for many years any objective analysis of the person and the role of Luther himself. As one of the great influences on the course of modern religious and secular history, Luther has been lauded as a liberator and castigated as a traitor.

Historical Evaluation

Soon after his death men like Dürer and Malanchthon called Luther "the dove of the Holy Spirit." Protestant panegyrists praised him generally as the swan prophesied by John Huss, the angel of the Apocalypse and the fifth Evangelist, but his Catholic adversaries saw him as an angry friar who defied authority and burdened the Church with heresy. In Grobianist terms he was treated as "the son of the devil," and "that Saxon pig," while Thomas More, in the idiom of the day, referred to Luther as "furiosum fraterculum et latrinarium nebulonem cum suis merdis et stercoribus cacantem cacatumque."

This first phase of defiant vilification was succeeded by the periods of Pietism and the Enlightenment when Catholic interest in Luther almost disappeared except for occasional oratorical outbursts by the Jesuits, Bellarmine and Becanus, and the more conciliatory concern of Bishop Bossuet. The Council of Trent condemned what it conceived to be Luther's doctrines and he was henceforth known chiefly in Catholic circles as one of the heretical adversaries of a long list of dogmatic declarations.

Late in the 19th century Leo XIII's opening of the Vatican archives, the foundation of the German Institute in Rome, and especially the influence of Leopold von Ranke rekindled a sense of the importance of the historical development of Christianity. Earlier in the 19th century Johann Görres had claimed that Luther had ruined German culture and that the defects of the Church would have been gradually corrected without his revolt. Ignaz von Döllinger later insisted that Luther had involved Germany in the Thirty Years' War and was responsible for her subsequent internal disorders. Johann Janssen, on the other hand, claimed that Luther had preceded and actually caused the decadence in Germany.

By the turn of the 20th century, historical oversimplification was the great crime of both

sides, as Protestants and Catholics searching for
an identity sought out and cited sources to sub-
stantiate their preconceived hypotheses. The
quadricentennial of Luther's birth occasioned a
resurgence of Protestant interest in the German
friar and found its best expression in the monu-
mental Weimar edition of his writings. Catholic
irritation at this revival was especially marked
in the work of the Dominican, Heinrich Denifle.
In 1903 he attempted to demythologize Luther
by discrediting him even as an original heretic
and by castigating him as a friar who elaborated
the doctrine of salvation by faith alone into an
apology for his own weakness and inability to
fulfill his religious vows.

In 1910 the Jesuit, Hartmann Grisar, condemned certain excesses of Denifle but, despite
a token sympathy with some of Luther's writings
still concentrated on the reformer's troubled conscience, his marriage with the nun, Catherine von
Bora, the exhortation to the princes to extermi-
nate the peasants in 1525 and his complicity in
the bigamous marriage of Philip of Hesse. Denifle
had concentrated on the historical aspects of
Luther's doctrine, but Grisar treated Luther as a
man altogether deplorable and sick, governed by
a pathological megalomania. Until recently, even
in scholarly Catholic circles the Denifle-Grisar
judgment remained standard. Even Jacques
Maritain, in his concern over Luther's influence
on the disruption of cultural unity and on the
formation of the modern conscience, fell into the
pitfalls of this historical interpretation. In his
eagerness to pinpoint Luther's tragedy, Maritain
accepted uncritically the standard assumptions

and used them to show how Luther's powerful and impulsive nature was divested of all measure by a disastrous egocentrism.

Historical Re-Evaluation

In our own time the crucible of events, especially in Germany under a pagan Nazi regime, forced Christians of both confessions to re-evaluate their respective positions. Catholic revisionist historiography has been sparked especially by the renowned Church historian Joseph Lortz, with his open admiration for Luther's theology of the cross, his trust in God and his dependence on Scripture. Lortz insisted that Luther must be seen in his setting of Hapsburg-Valois dynastic rivalries, the ambitions of German duchies and the great need of reform in a Church still burdened with the abuses of the Avignon period, the confusion of the Great Schism, and the enervating forces of the Medicean Renaissance.

Lortz admits that in the 16th century there was valid ground for criticism of the Church with its exaggerated clericalism and worldliness but that Luther's action against these weaknesses turned out to be not reform, but rejection. The incompetency of men like Eck in dealing with Luther, the poor quality of the prevalent Occamist theology and the general failure of Churchmen to take the religious motives of the reformers seriously, are all part of what Lortz considers causes for a Catholic sense of guilt regarding the Reformation. Even so, Luther cut loose the mooring lines of a burdensome authority and thereby deprived himself of the strength of an objective teaching Church, a sacramental priesthood and the fund of Christian tradition.

For Lortz, Luther became an exaggerated subjectivist so involved with his personal commitment to God that he neglected the successful implementation of Christianity. As a result, Luther failed to subsume the subjective factors of religious experience within norms set by an objective supra-personal authority. Luther thus set up a personalist structure of religion with man and his experience as the primary focus.

Johannes Hessen, in 1947, went even further than Lortz. He rejected Lortz's main thesis of Luther's subjectivism and showed Luther as an Old Testament prophet inveighing against intellectualism, moralism, sacramentalism and institutionalism. While still insisting on the teaching office of the Church and admitting that Luther went too far in his struggle, Hessen insists that Luther's message is of guiding importance for contemporary Catholicism. The well-known Jesuit Erich Przywara also defended several of the most important ideas of Lutheran scholarship against Lortz's thesis regarding Luther's basic subjectivism.

Luther and Catholic Historians

To offset the Rankean conclusion that the Counter-Reformation was caused by the Reformation, certain Catholic historians have insisted on referring to these two phases as the Protestant Revolt and the Catholic Restoration. Men like Pierre Janelle and Leon Cristiani, while admitting a certain catalytic value to Luther's role, claimed that there were strong forces of reform within the Church itself regardless of Luther. This judgment has come under serious attack by scholars who note that the *devotio moderna* was limited to the Netherlands and parts of northern France and Germany, that the social reforms of Sts. Bernardine and Catherine touched only a segment of northern Italy and the revival under Ximenes was landlocked behind the Pyrenees.

The overwhelming fact is that despite the acknowledged need for sweeping corporate reform, the episcopate and the papacy in the century before Luther could not or did not reform. Hubert Jedin, the expert on the Council of Trent, warns us that not only were the dogmatic definitions of that Council elicited by the errors of the Reformers, but even its reform decrees might never have been promulgated without the stimulus of the Protestant revolt.

Friedrich Richter, a Lutheran minister before entering Catholicism, sees the hand of Providence in permitting the Reformation. Historically, the Reformation, as seen by Richter, was necessary to set in action a reform movement, even within the Church, which was long overdue. For Richter, Luther, like Ignatius, was a hero of unity and the German friar was motivated by a genuine desire to reform the entire Church, not to encourage a proliferation of religious bodies.

Adolf Herte, meanwhile, after an analysis of five hundred works by Catholics discovered that, almost without exception, all of them are seriously dependent on the writings of the 16th-century Canon Johann Dobendeck, who is more generally known as Cochläus. This humanist turned controversialist wrote over two hundred books, including his famous biography of Luther in 1549, which vividly convey his distaste for the non-humanist Luther. In Cochläus' polemics may be found all the charges that have become so dominant in the Catholic's popular conception of the German reformer. The still extensive, uncritical use of such a source should cause nothing but shame.

By 1950, in France, Yves Congar was referring to the Reformation as something that has addressed and is still addressing the Roman Church with important questions. Accepting the Catholics' share of responsibility for the 16th-century tragedy, Congar shows how not only the heresy but also the legitimate part of the Reformation protest have been too often repudiated. Still, Congar criticizes Luther for his onesidedness in driving home a single idea from the Epistle to the Galatians. For Congar, Luther, like Marcion earlier, claimed he wanted to restore the Church to its original form, but he did so by cutting off vital parts of its tradition. Luther is also criticized for his somewhat spiritualistic concept of the Church, which prevented him from accepting the divinely established visible structure manifested in the continuity of the apostolic ministry.

Luther's Theological Writings

Catholic scholars have recently turned more and more to an examination of Luther's own theological writings. It is in Luther's non-polemical works that Louis Bouyer finds that for Luther "by faith alone" no more excludes works proceeding from faith than the Council of Trent will accept works which are not themselves the products of saving grace received by faith as the cause of salvation. For Bouyer, Luther's concept of salvation, properly understood, is in perfect harmony with Catholic tradition, conciliar definitions and St. Thomas. Bouyer has further attempted to correct a common Catholic misunderstanding by showing that Protestants do not look upon Luther so much as a saint and a model in every detail of his life and teaching but, rather, admire the manner in which, at a certain period of his life, he resolved a particular problem.

The Dominican, Thomas M. McDonough, has recently investigated the relationship of the Law and the Gospel in Luther and concluded that, while not traditionally scholastic, Luther does operate within the despair-faith experience of daily Christian existence and it is only in such a framework that we can comprehend the various labels and paradoxes commonly attributed to his theology.

Lortz, Jedin, Herte, Richter and Bouyer are representative of a new Catholic scholarship which views Luther less as a villain bent on the violent disruption of Christ's body and more as one searching for religious conviction who became eventually a catalyst for real reform within the Church. This reflects an existentialist approach that side-steps problems involving the static structures connected with Christian revelation and focuses rather, on the purpose for which the structure exists, namely, on the dynamism involved in grace and salvation.

The renaissance of scholarship about Luther places us in a far more secure position as to an accurate understanding of what really happened than, for example, the debate-conscious 16th century. This is largely due to the phenomenon of ecumenism with its fruitful interchange of insight and understanding. The recent publication and subsequent popularity of several volumes of articles drawn from diverse sources from both sides of the Christian Curtain are stark evidence of a deepening unanimity.

Hans Küng, for example, in his careful study of Karl Barth's treatment of Luther concludes that there was no opposition between Luther and Trent. Luther underlines the divine uncreated elements while Trent stressed the human, created aspects. For both, it is always and ultimately God who through Christ reinstates man to friendship with Himself by an act that is absolutely gratuitous.

For Catholic scholarship to have come so far in its re-evaluation of Luther has proven an incentive to Protestant scholars to re-examine their own experience. Unfortunately, such historical re-evaluation has been mainly confined to the more advanced theological circles in Germany and France. Much of the English - speaking Church is still being fed on the misconceptions and misrepresentations of the Denifle-Grisar tradition. At least in some areas, at some levels, Church historians as well as theologians have abandoned polemics and have become involved in the excitement of talking with one another concerning the manifold significance of Martin Luther.

18

The Inner Testimony
of the Spirit

Stanley Kutz

ONE of the recent trends in Catholic theology
which must surely bring joy to the hearts of
other Christians and perhaps anxiety to the
hearts of some Catholics, is the renewed interest
in and emphasis upon the role of the Holy Spirit
in the Christian life. The Protestant may see
herein a vindication of the pneumatic-personalist
view which his faith has always emphasized. The
Catholic may experience a vague sense of betrayal
of positions heroically defended by his spiritual
forbears.

It may be salutary, then, for both sides to be
reminded that this movement in Catholic theology is not quite as revolutionary as it appears
at first sight, but is rather a renewed emphasis
on what has always been present in the most
authentic Catholic tradition. To illustrate this
point, we propose to sketch only one aspect of

the question as treated by one witness of the Christian tradition—the role of the Holy Spirit in the genesis of faith, as treated by St. Thomas Aquinas.

Needless to say, St. Thomas emphasizes quite adequately the role of the visible Church and of her human ministers in the spreading of the Gospel. But this, at least in principle, has never been a source of dissension among divided Christians; all have agreed that faith comes from hearing, and that if men are to hear the good news, someone must announce it to them. It is rather in determining the extent of the real efficacy of this human ministry of the divine Word that differences have arisen, and opposition has become bitter.

In the past, Protestants have judged Catholic catechesis as relying too heavily, or perhaps even exclusively, on human instrumentality, on human authority and argumentation, thus evacuating the mysterious efficacy of God's merciful Word to man, and man's free and personal response to that Word. They saw little evidence that Catholic catechists truly believed that it is God's Spirit, the Spirit of Truth, who teaches us all things and brings to our remembrance all that Christ has said to us (*cf.* John 14, 26). They have had, perhaps, a special dread of those "arguments of suitability" of the scholastic theologians which seemed to substitute rational arguments for the mystery of God's personal and salvific love. What does St. Thomas, greatest of the scholastics and perhaps the cleverest of all the men who have tried to show the reasonability of the Christian faith, have to say on this matter?

St. Thomas on Faith

He tells us, first of all, that it is the Holy Spirit who breathes faith into man: "The justice of God comes through faith in Jesus Christ. This faith comes not from man, but from the Holy Spirit, who breathes it into man, as we are told in Romans 8, 15: 'You have received the spirit of sons, by virtue of which we cry: Abba, Father'" (*In Gal.* V, 5).

This basic theme is expressed in a variety of ways by Thomas Aquinas, but nowhere more clearly than when he comes to contrast the Old and the New Dispensations. He is at pains to point out that whereas the Old Covenant was a law of the letter, imposed on servants from without, the New Covenant consists precisely in interior profusion of the Holy Spirit, whereby we are transformed into sons of God, and invited to a free and personal response as becomes children of a loving Father. The Old Law was imperfect because it consisted only in commands externally imposed, without providing the interior illumination and strength to fulfill them; thus it could not give life, but was indeed the occasion of death, for it made transgression conscious, without providing the means of avoiding it.

In direct contrast the New Law is perfect, precisely because it consists in the interior pouring forth of the Holy Spirit, whereby we become conscious of our divine adoption, and thus proceed to accomplish God's will of our own initiative, out of gratitude for the love shown us. It is no longer a question of precepts externally imposed, but of personal love responding to Per-

sonal Love, made posible by the pouring forth
in the hearts of Christ's faithful of the Holy
Spirit, who is the Person of Love in the Trinity.
Aquinas' thought on this point receives its most
radical expression when he says: "Even the
words of the Gospel would bring death (as did
the Law of the Old Testament) unless they were
accompanied by the interior healing grace of
faith" (*Summa Theol.* I-II, 106, 2; *cf.* the whole
tract on the New Covenant; I-II, 106-108).

It would be unrealistic to expect of St. Thomas
a detailed tract on the relation of the Holy Spirit
to the reading of the Scriptures. The emphasis of
the Reformers on the peculiar efficacy of the
Scriptures when they are read "in the Spirit" is
conceivable only in a world which possessed the
printing press. On at least one occasion, however, Aquinas does touch on this question. Commenting on the veil which St. Paul says covers
the hearts of the Jews when Moses is read to
them, he attributes this spiritual blindness to the
fact that the Jews had not received the Holy
Spirit, Author of the law of liberty: "Because
the Spirit is Lord, he can give us the liberty to
use the Scriptures of the Old Testament without
(their being covered by) a veil. And those who
do not possess the Holy Spirit cannot thus freely
use them" (*In II Cor.*, III, 17).

St. Thomas on Conscience

We find an interesting word on the dignity of
personal conscience and its confirmation by the
Holy Spirit when Thomas comments on Romans
9, 1: "I am speaking the truth in Christ, I am

not lying; my conscience bears me witness in the Holy Spirit."

Aquinas notes that the saints have three infallible witnesses to the truth they utter, namely Christ, who is Truth, secondly their own conscience, and finally the Holy Spirit, who preserves their conscience from the possibility of error. (In another context, commenting on 2 Cor. 1, 12, Thomas tells us that "man ought always to rely more on the witness of his own conscience concerning himself than on the witness of others.") And if we ask how the Holy Spirit bears witness to our own spirit or conscience, Aquinas replies that this takes place not by any external sound addressed to man's ears, as the Father bore witness to the Son (Matt. 3, 17), but rather the Holy Spirit renders witness to our spirit through the experience of filial love he creates in us (*cf. In Rom.* VIII, 16).

One final text ought to make abundantly clear St. Thomas' position on the primacy of the Holy Spirit in the genesis of saving faith in our hearts. Commenting on Christ's promise of the Spirit, "who will teach you all things," he remarks: "Whatever man may teach externally, he labors in vain unless the Holy Spirit provides interior understanding; for unless the Spirit were present to the heart of the hearer, the words of the teacher would be idle; and this is true to such an extent, that even the Son, speaking through the instrument of his humanity, would accomplish nothing, unless he himself also worked interiorly, through the Holy Spirit" (*In Joann.* XIV, 26).

This clear teaching on the inner testimony of the Holy Spirit in the conversion of men to the life of faith, by one whom the Catholic Church honors as the greatest of her doctors, ought to reassure modern Catholic theologians that their attempt to bring out the role of the Spirit in the genesis of faith and the whole moral life of the Christian, is in no way an innovation but rather the return to the fullness of the Catholic tradition.

19

Ecumenical Reflection on Penance

Stanley Kutz

BEFORE the opening of the Vatican Council Pope John published the encyclical, *Paenitentiam agere*, to remind the Catholic people that the Ecumenical Council is a spiritual event in the life of the Church which must be prepared in a spiritual way. "If we consult the books of the Old and New Testaments," the Pope wrote, "we recognize that whenever God has deigned to manifest himself to men in a more solemn manner—to speak in human terms—he first called them to prayer and penance." So it is with this Ecumenical Council. The Catholic people must make room in their midst for the action of the Holy Spirit. Pope John advocated Christian penance "the instrument of purification and spiritual renewal."

Pope John's Ecumenical Approach

Though penance has been an area of contro-

versy between Catholics and Protestants for
many centuries, the ecumenical approach of our
day may well give rise to fruitful dialogue on the
subject. We shall follow the Pope in his argument. According to the Christian Gospel, the
fundamental renewal of man takes place in the
baptism of faith. It is there that, in spite of our
sins, Christ takes pity on us, forgives our sins
and identifies himself with us in his holiness. We
are made beautiful in Christ, and our sins no
longer exist. The Pope quotes from St. Paul:
"Christ loved the Church and delivered himself
for her, that he might sanctify her, cleansing her
in the bath of water by means of the word"
(Eph. 5, 26). And yet, even after our baptism,
we continue to commit sins and revolt against
the will of God. But, because we have become
brothers of Christ and share, by faith, in his
vitality, we are able to cooperate in the reception
of the forgiveness which the merciful Father
grants us for the sake of his Son. This cooperation, engendered, borne and completed by faith
and grace, we call Christian penance.

The Pope gave a definition of the Church's
holiness that leaves ample room for the sins and
faults of the Catholic community. He wrote:
"The Church, the beloved Spouse of her divine
Savior, has always kept herself holy and immacu-
late in the faith which enlightens her, in the
sacraments that nourish her, in the laws and
precepts that govern her, and in the many members who adorn her with the beauty of heroic
virtues." The Church, therefore, is holy because
of what Christ does in her. She is holy because
of the divine gifts, and the fruits produced by

them in her children. But, besides this unalienable sanctity, there is in her infidelity and selfishness, and for the sake of these we are asked to do penance.

Penance and Scripture

To establish the need of penance and to inspire the Catholic people to enter into it with the right spirit, Pope John quoted at length from the Scriptures, from the Old and New Testaments. He did not, however, enter upon the difficulties raised by the traditional Protestant objections to penance. While Christians agree that in the Old Testament penance played an important part in reconciling the people of Israel with their God, they do not see eye to eye in regard to penance in the New Testament. Christ has offered himself once and for all as propitiation for the sins of men, and hence the need for further acts of penance does not seem obvious to many Protestant readers of the Gospel.

The biblical passages quoted by John XXIII may be divided into three sections. The first set (Matt. 3, 1-2; 4, 17; Luke 13, 5; Acts 2, 38) recalls that, from the beginning, the proclamation of the kingdom was accompanied by the call for repentance. "Repent, for the kingdom of God is at hand." This was the cry of John the Baptist. But it was also the call of Jesus himself, in whom the kingdom becomes present to us (*cf.* Luke 17, 21) and that of the apostles announcing the Gospel to the people. The recognition of our sins and, consequently, our need for redemption, was the prerequisite for receiving the gift of faith. Yet the call for repentance has meaning not only at the entrance into the new life, it retains its meaning and its urgency throughout the entire Christian life; in fact, it takes on new quality after baptism.

This becomes clear in a second set of passages (Matt. 11, 12; Luke 9, 23; Rom. 14, 17-18; 1 Cor. 9, 27): that those who follow Christ must deny themselves and take up their cross daily. Having received the Holy Spirit we are to leave the way of the flesh (selfishness) and walk in the way of the Spirit. Reborn in Christ man must forever break in himself, with the Spirit to help him, the tendencies proper to his wounded nature; he must put to death the works of the old man in order to make more room, with the help of grace, for the works of the new man. Without doing some violence to himself no man will be a faithful follower of Jesus.

A third set of passages (Gal. 5, 27; Col. 1, 24; 1 Peter 3, 18) shows that the meaning of this struggle is not a moral, but a properly religious one. It belongs to the order of faith. The purpose of our renewed ways is to conform us more closely to the image of Jesus, who suffered and died for us so that we may live. Repentance and the penance that flows from it are works of Christ in us, impressing upon us his own likeness. Joining our sacrifices to his own unrepeatable self-surrender on the cross, Christ renders fruitful the works of those who belong to him.

Protestants and Fasting

The Catholic understanding of these scriptural themes may give rise to a dialogue with Protestant Christians. It is well-known that, traditionally, Protestants have rejected the religious use of fasting and other forms of self-limitation. To speak of penance, satisfaction, mortification, good works and sacrifices is a horror to the ears of many Protestants since to them these practices seem to belittle or even deny the very heart of the Christian Gospel, namely that Jesus has once and for all sacrificed himself for all of mankind. In him all human sins are atoned for. This we must believe. In fact, to enter upon the forgiveness of sins, this is what we must believe. According to this Protestant interpretation, we must accept that Christ has done everything for us, confess that we do not deserve it and are unable to do anything in the eyes of God which brings us nearer to him. For many Protestants, "good works" are not only useless but even dangerous to salvation because a man could be tempted to put confidence in his own doing and, through that, fail to discover his own impotence which is the prerequisite for the total surrender to Christ in faith.

If we look at the ordinary Protestant commentaries on the Scriptures — except the most recent ones — we are amazed at the one-sided apologetical manner in which they treat the New Testament doctrine of fasting. (We, too, of course, have our own touchy spots where, in the past, we have interpreted scriptural passages under an apologetical strain.)

Prayer and Fasting in the New Testament

For the New Testament, prayer and fasting go hand in hand (*cf.* Matt. 17, 20; Mark 9, 28; Luke 2, 37; Acts 10, 31; 1 Cor. 7, 5). While

Jesus condemned hypocritical fasting (Matt. 6, 16) and Paul opposed gnostic dualism which saw evil in the things of the body (Rom. 14, 14; 1 Tim. 4, 3; Titus 1, 15), we hear of no criticism of the ancient biblical practices of fasting, almsgiving, and other forms of voluntary self-denial. From the beginning fasting was linked to the liturgy of the Christian community (*cf.* Acts 13, 2-3; 14, 22). The attitude of the early Christians is well expressed in the answer of Jesus to the followers of the Baptist questioning why his disciples did not fast. Jesus said: "Can the wedding guests mourn as long as the bridegroom is with them? But the days will come when the bridegroom shall be taken away from them, and then they will fast" (Matt. 9, 15; *cf.* Mark 2, 19-20). While the early Church had a keen sense of the risen Christ's presence in the community and hence expressed great joy in its liturgical worship, repentance remained part of the Gospel even then.

The ordinary Protestant commentary of Scripture did not face these texts squarely. Often the commentator claimed that many of the verses cited above were later additions. This is certainly a possibility, but would have to be proven. Yet even if these verses were insertions, they express all the more forcefully the faith and practice of the early Christian community. Other commentators spend their effort in explaining what these passages do *not* mean: this happens especially in regard to Colossians 1, 24.

Catholics, however, are not without guilt in producing this Protestant attitude. The reason why Protestants reacted so vehemently against

fasting and other penitential exercises was, to a
large extent, the unevangelical way in which we
spoke about, and practiced, "good works." In
many of our spiritual and theological books, in
sermons, and religious literature in general we
have spoken about penance as if it were our work
to pacify the God whom we have offended, or
worse, to make satisfaction for other people's
offenses against him. But had not Jesus done
all this once and for all? Preaching Christian
penance we did not always announce, in the same
breath, that personal sacrifices are meaningful
only because they are offered in Christ, that they
are the fruit of Christ's grace in us, that we can
offer them precisely because we are redeemed by
his unique and all-sufficient sacrifice, and that
they are precious to the eternal Father because
he recognizes in them gestures of his only-begotten Son.

On the other hand, classical Protestantism
emphasized (over-emphasized, in Catholic eyes)
that the total life of the Christian is constantly
qualified by repentance. The Reformers rejected
penance, not because it gave expression to a
repentance for which there was no room in the
life of the redeemed, but on the contrary because
in their eyes it seemed to replace true repentance. External observances seemed to substitute
for the contrition of the heart. There is, undoubtedly, a real danger here. Of this Catholics
are much aware. Pope John wrote: "Exterior
forms of penance would be useless unless they
were accompanied by an inner cleansing of the
soul and sincere remorse for one's sins." Penance
is always, in the first place, a divine doing in us.

Positive Attitude Toward Penance

Today there is much evidence that Protestant theological writers are gaining a more positive understanding of Christian penance. The biblical commentaries have changed their tone. The article "Fasting," in *Vocabulary of the Bible* (Lutterworth Press, London, 1958) gives an open-minded, though reserved, account of the New Testament teaching. The article "Fasten" in *Die Religion in Geschichte und Gegenwart* (3rd edition, Tübingen, 1958) describes the biblical attitude toward fasting with even greater freedom.

What is more important still is that the biblical conception of man as an indivisible physico-spiritual unity, emphasized in all modern scriptural commentaries, gives us a deeper understanding of what the older Protestant authors contemptuously described as "external works."

If man is one, the contrition of the heart must express itself in visible deeds. If we are sorry, we want to show that we are sorry. In fact, man being what he is, we suspect the sincerity of declared remorse if we do not see it expressed in physical deeds. While many Protestant writers reach out for a more positive attitude toward penance, not many will go as far as the Presbyterian theologian G. MacGregor, in his *The Coming Reformation*, (The Westminster Press, Philadelphia, 1960) in a chapter called "The Revival of Discipline."

The question of penance is an area worthy of further study. If Catholic piety must relearn to appreciate the divine doing in penance, Protestants may have to discover the necessity of making repentance incarnate in the new life brought by Christ. This is more than a theoretical question. If, indeed, conformity to Christ implies a certain voluntary share in his humiliation, then without this obedience to the Lord the ecumenical movement will not advance.

20

The Conditional
Re-Baptism of Anglicans

Walton Hannah

THE practice of universal indiscriminate baptism *sub conditione* of Anglicans entering the Catholic Church who can produce an Anglican baptismal certificate arose in England from motives unhappily other than entirely theological, and has spread since to other countries where Anglicanism is to be found. For instance, in England (1956) a High Church Anglican clergyman, the Rev. Hugh Ross Williamson, was received into the Church together with his wife and small son. The latter had been baptized by his father with the full Roman form and ceremonies, and with the correct intention, but a conditional baptism was nevertheless insisted on, despite the father's protests, "in order to get it on the record," that is, in a Catholic baptismal register. No doubts whatsoever were expressed as to the validity of the former baptism.

Anglican Baptismal Service

It is well-known that the Anglican Church has a fixed liturgy in the Book of Common Prayer, 1662, which is the norm for Anglican worship and sacraments throughout the entire Anglican communion, though different ecclesiastical Provinces, including Canada, have their own local versions.

The variations between "high church" and "low church" Anglicans are concerned mainly with the forms of public worship; that is, morning and evening prayer, and particularly the communion service, where individual ministers do indeed take considerable liberties in their use of the official liturgy. High church and low church alike, however, teach the necessity of infant baptism, and universally use the form provided in the Anglican Prayer Book. A very few extreme high churchmen may supplement it with ceremonies of chrism and salt taken from the Roman ritual. But except for this tiny minority the Prayer Book baptismal service is universally adhered to.

The form of baptism in the Prayer Book of the Anglican Church in Canada is verbatim the same as in the 1662 Prayer Book of the Church of England. The service begins with the exhortation:

"Dearly beloved, forasmuch as all men are conceived and born in sin, and that our Saviour Christ saith, None can enter into the kingdom of God, except he be regenerate and born anew of water and of the Holy Ghost, I beseech you to call upon God the Father, through Our Lord Jesus Christ, that of His bounteous mercy He will grant to this child that thing which by nature he cannot have, that he may be baptized with water and the Holy Ghost, and received into Christ's holy Church, and be made a living member of the same."

The following prayers commemorate the salvation of Noah in the ark, the passing of the Children of Israel through the Red Sea, and the baptism in the Jordan in which God sanctified "water to the mystical washing away of sin" and assured "that he, coming to thy holy baptism, may receive remission of his sins by spiritual regeneration . . . that this infant may enjoy the everlasting benediction of thy heavenly washing and may come to the eternal kingdom."

Then follows the reading of St. Mark's Gospel and an exhortation. Then the sponsors in the name of the infant renounce the world, the flesh, and the devil, and assent to the Apostles' Creed in the interrogative form, and profess their desire for baptism in that faith.

After a few more prayers follows the actual baptism.

"Then the priest shall take the child into his hands, and shall say to the godfathers and godmothers: 'Name this Child.' And then naming it after them (if they shall certify him that the child may well endure it) he shall dip it in the water discreetly and warily, saying, 'N (ame), I baptize thee in the Name of the Father, and of the Son, and of the Holy Ghost. Amen.' But if they certify that the child is weak, it shall suffice to pour water upon it, saying the aforesaid words.'"

The latter form, that is, pouring rather than immersion, is now the universal Anglican practice. It will be noted that sprinkling is not allowed.

These extracts show that the Anglican baptismal service is not only valid as regards form and matter, but also teaches the full Catholic doctrine that baptismal regeneration cleanses from original sin and makes the baptized sons of God and members of Christ.

Anglican Teaching on Baptism

The Anglican teaching on baptism is further set forth in the official catechism, which is also printed in the Book of Common Prayer for the Anglican Church in Canada. Here we are told:

"A sacrament is an outward and visible sign of an inward and spiritual grace given unto us, ordained by Christ himself," and that "the outward and visible sign of baptism is water, wherein a person is baptized in the name of the Father and of the Son and of the Holy Ghost." The inward and spiritual grace is described as "a death unto sin, and a new birth unto righteousness; for being by nature born in sin, and the children of wrath, we are hereby made the children of grace."

Of lesser authority in the eyes of most Anglican theologians than the Prayer Book itself as a statement of doctrine are the Thirty-nine Articles of Religion to which Anglican clerics swear at least a general assent. Article XXVII is on baptism. It reads:

"Baptism is not only a sign of profession, and mark of difference, whereby Christian men are discerned from others that be not christened, but it is also a sign of regeneration or new birth, whereby, as by an instrument, they that receive Baptism rightly are grafted into the Church; the promises of the forgiveness of sin, and of our adoption to be the Sons of God by the Holy Ghost, are visibly signed and sealed; Faith is confirmed, and Grace increased by virtue of prayer unto God. The Baptism of young children is in any wise to be retained in the Church as most agreeable with the institution of Christ."

These, then, are the official forms and doctrinal statements of the Anglican Church on baptism which, it is submitted, are Catholic in teaching and valid in administration. It is alleged, and with some truth, that there are Modernists in the Anglican Communion who, while complying with the above form and matter in administering baptism, do not accept the doctrine of original sin or baptismal regeneration therefrom, and therefore have an imperfect intention. However, even the most extreme Modernist regards baptism as the rite of entry into the congregation of Christ's Church, and the unanimous opinion of Catholic moral theologians is that faulty and even heretical views on the nature of baptism do not invalidate the sacrament if properly administered; the Anglican Modernist certainly has the intention *facere quod facit Ecclesia* however minimist his personal views on the Rite and what the Church means thereby.

Validity of Baptism outside the Church

From the most ancient times, the Catholic Church has respected baptism as valid given outside her borders, even when the ministers or the recipients of baptism did not hold the Catholic faith. This principle gave rise to a controversy in the 3rd century. A practice, introduced and recommended by the Church of North Africa, of rebaptizing those who had received baptism from heretical ministers, was condemned by the Roman Church in the person of Pope Stephan I. (*See* Denz. 46, 47.)

This doctrine was put in the most formal language at the Council of Trent.

"If anyone says that the baptism, which is given by heretics in the name of the Father and of the Son and of the Holy Ghost, with the intention of doing what the Church does, is not true baptism: let him be anathema" (Denz. 860).

In March, 1570, the Congregation of the Council made the declaration:

"This Synod teaches that the baptism of the Calvinists is valid and that therefore those who are baptized by them are not to be baptized again. For the Calvinists seceded from the Church not over the matter of baptism, and have preserved, even if not the solemnity, so at least the ecclesiastical form." (This was ratified by Pius V on June 19, 1570.)

The Councils at Evreux (1576), Rouen (1581) and Cambrai (1587) confirmed this decision and rendered it more precise. At Evreux we hear:

"Pius V defined that the baptism of Calvinists is true since they use the form and matter instituted by Christ with the general intention to do what Christ has instituted, even if they err in the particular interpretation and special intention" (Fontes I.C. IV, No 871, pp 153-54).

At Cambrai it was decided that conditional baptism should be administered only in cases where the form had not been observed.

Bellarmine interpreted the Tridentine formula "with the intention of doing what the Church does" *(faciendi quod facit Ecclesia)* as follows:

"The Council of Trent . . . did not say that the minister of baptism had to intend what the Church intends, but only what the Church does. What the Church does, moreover, expresses the action performed, not the end sought thereby" (De Sacramentis in Genere, I, Ch. 27).

Every subsequent reply of the Holy Office to *dubia* on baptismal validity appears to be based on this interpretation of intention: the one thing that counts in this issue is the correct observance of matter and form of the sacrament.

Baptism of Ministers Denying Catholic Doctrine

Since we are only dealing with Anglican baptisms there is no need to go into the question of doctrinal conformity in the minister giving the baptism. It is nevertheless interesting to note that according to the constant teaching of the Catholic Church the baptism of men who specifically deny the Catholic doctrine on baptism is nevertheless regarded as valid. There is, for instance, the classical decree of the Holy Office, November 20, 1878 (Denz. 1848). This question was sent to the Holy Office: Whether baptism should be conferred conditionally on heretics who are converted to the Catholic religion, from whatever locality they come, and to whatever sect they pertain? The answer was negative. Then the proper procedure is described. There should be an examination as to whether the baptism given in the sect had been valid. If the baptism has been given validly, then the convert should be received through a profession of faith only. If it has not been validly administered, then the convert should be baptized unconditionally. But if the investigation finds no evidence for or against the validity of baptism, or if a reasonable doubt exists regarding validity, then the convert should be baptized conditionally. It is stated that the conditional baptism should be performed privately or secretly, presumably in order to avoid the impression that the Church was rebaptizing, and therefore Donatist, in her practice.

We shall also quote the famous "Oceania Case." Some natives in Central Oceania had been baptized by Methodist missionaries and the following *dubium* was proposed to the Holy Office in 1872, on their conversion to the Catholic Church: "Whether baptism administered by these heretics is doubtful on account of defect of intention to do what Christ willed, if an express declaration was made by the minister before he baptized, that baptism had no effect on the soul?" The answer was: "In the negative, since despite the error about the effects of baptism, the intention of doing what the Church does is not excluded" (A.S.S. XXV, 246).

The doctrine and approved practice of the Catholic Church is quite clear: every baptism in water and the name of the Holy Trinity is valid.

Indiscriminate Conditional Baptism Condemned

For many years it has been the invariable custom of Catholic priests in Egypt, both of Coptic and Latin rite, to rebaptize conditionally with no previous inquiry, all converts from the Abyssinian Coptic Church. The form and matter and intention as expressed in the Abyssinian ritual were adequate and valid, but the practice of re-baptism became general because of certain alleged careless practices in administering the sacrament. At a Council in Cairo on May 1, 1960, however, His Excellency Msgr. Amand Hubert, Latin Vicar-Apostolic of Heliopolis, cited Holy Office decrees on Abyssinian baptisms issued in 1741, 1856, 1860 and 1866. The last expressly condemned a decree of the then Vicar-Apostolic ordering the indiscriminate conditional re-baptism of all Abyssinian converts.

Here is an excerpt from the condemnation: "The decree on indiscriminate re-baptism *sub conditione* of all who were baptized by the schismatics in Ethiopia is not approved of by the Eminent Fathers. Everyone knows that baptism given by schismatic or heretical ministers is valid as long as nothing is left out which the Roman Church has prescribed about matter, form and intention, and that such baptisms cannot be repeated, even *sub conditione*, without grave sin and the pain of irregularity, unless a reasonable doubt exists concerning the invalidity of the baptism."

In spite of this very clear text, however, indiscriminate conditional re-baptisms continued in Egypt until Msgr. Hubert enforced the Holy Office decree, on May 1, 1960, and insisted on an examination of validity in the case of each convert. In a great number of cases since, the inquiry has concluded for the validity of the Abyssinian baptism. (A very full account of this appears in *Parole et Mission*, Vol. 11, Oct., 1960, pp. 380-591, by Fr. Clement, S.J.)

Anglican Baptisms

The above remarks are surely relevant to the situation in many countries where Anglicans joining the Catholic Church are conditionally baptized without any inquiry, even when they produce their Anglican baptismal certificate. Catholic theologians have not been wanting who have strongly criticized the common practice.

While it is true that baptism is administered rather carelessly in some of the Protestant communions, especially on the North American continent (though even here a careful examination of the situation is required), this should not influence the Catholic attitude toward the baptisms given in the Anglican Church. Especially in our own day, when the ecumenical movement has made us appreciate more deeply the bond among Christians created by baptism, an ecclesiastical practice more in harmony with Catholic teaching would convince Anglicans that we take the baptismal bond seriously and teach Catholics to regard as brothers, even if separated, those who have been reborn in the baptism of faith.

In this spirit we find the ruling in the new French *Directoire pour les Actes administratifs des Sacrements:* It is not permitted to confer, or repeat, conditional baptism by simple scruple or systematically to avoid searching for a written or oral proof of the baptism (Nos. 81-86).

It is interesting to note in this connection that in the last century the baptisms in the Anglican Church of Mother Seton and Cardinal Newman were acknowledged at their reception into the Catholic Church: no conditional baptismal ceremony was imposed on them.

21

Birth Regulation in Ecumenical Perspective

Stanley Kutz

IT is admitted by all that the authenticity of ecumenical encounter depends as much on the acknowledgment of differences as on the search for points of agreement between separated Christians. Nevertheless, there is one area of patent disagreement which has remained notably absent from the dialogue—the area of marital ethics, and especially the problem of contraception. Whether on account of natural reticence, or because they fear arriving at a total impasse, the partners of the Catholic-Protestant dialogue tend instinctively to shy away from this question. There is much written and said on both sides, but it generally has more the character of polemic than of witness.

Assessing the Problem

Now this would seem to be a strange and unwarranted state of affairs. For what is at issue here is not so much a disagreement over the content and meaning of God's revelation but different ways of assessing the natural values associated with marriage. Since we presumably all share a common nature, open to the attraction of common values, one might hope for a truly fruitful exchange of conviction on this subject. But this hope seems doomed to frustration. The discussion is rarely undertaken, and almost never attains to the level of real communication. The Catholic immediately thinks of the rapid evolution which has taken place in Protestant conviction on this question, and censures his partner for "selling-out" traditional Christian values. The Protestant for his part believes that the Catholic is irrevocably committed to an irrational position which, for all its claims to be based on naturally perceptible values, must ultimately be defended with arguments from authority. The fact that those who exercise this authority in the Catholic Church are celibate only helps to convince the Protestant that no real dialogue is possible.

And yet we can surely not be content with this unfortunate state of affairs. What is the point of seeking a meeting of minds in the realm of lofty theological issues, if, at the level where the great majority of people live out the practical implications of their Christian commitment we are doomed to hopeless opposition and separation?

The question we must ask ourselves is whether or not the present state of the problem actually warrants the pessimistic attitude which both sides seem to take toward it. It seems to me that a second look will reveal to both partners areas where the discussion could profitably be initiated. This is not to say that one expects any easy agreement, any sudden change on either side. It is only to say that on a question where there already exists such community of experience it should be possible to profit from each other's understanding of the meaning of that experience. Let us now set forth some of the facts which give rise to this optimism.

Catholics Look at Protestants

The Catholic who listens to the witness of his Protestant friends will discover in them a concern for the same values which give meaning and substance to his own married life. He will learn (on the basis of partial sociological studies conducted in the U.S.) that they hope their marriage will be blessed with two or three children, an expectation which is somewhat lower than his own, but not drastically so. He will find them concerned about the moral and religious upbringing of their children, and shocked at the evidence of moral laxity in some segments of our society, as he himself is. He will discover, as Fr. Gerald Kelly, S.J. points out in an otherwise rather pessimistic article ("Christian unity and Christian marriage," *Theology Digest*, Winter, 1963), that there are some Anglicans and Protestants who entirely reject the use of contraceptives as a moral solution to the problems of Christian marriage. He will learn to distinguish the familial values cherished by most of his Protestant friends from the exaggerated statements of certain "liberals," even if these are occasionally ministers of religion. (He would not wish to have his own values judged on the basis of the grossly insensitive remarks of some of his co-religionists—including, occasionally, clerics). He will realize that he differs from his friends not so much in the area of values as of the most efficacious means of preserving and nourishing these values. In this context, an article by Fr. John A. O'Brien ("Family Planning in an Exploding Population," *Ave Maria*, Aug. 24, 1963, published simultaneously in the *Christian Century*), provides ample evidence of the growing Catholic awareness of the need for responsible parenthood "which is but another name for family planning " (p. 7).

Protestants Look at Catholics

On the other hand, the Protestant who is in contact with contemporary Catholic literature on the subject of marital ethics will discover a considerably more sophisticated and intellectually defensible position than he might have expected to find. He will note with satisfaction that married Catholics in increasing numbers and with growing articulation are witnessing to the hierarchy of marital values as they have experienced them in their own lives, and will see in this the possibility of communication on the basis of a common experience. He will observe that these expressions of conviction are printed in Catholic journals and magazines and are frequently accompanied by editorial comment of a positive nature. In this vein, one thinks of a number of articles that have appeared in the past few months in such national journals as *Jubilee* (De-

cember, 1963), *Commonweal* (Feb. 14, 1964)
and *Cross Currents* (Winter, 1964—a lengthy
article by Prof. Louis Dupré of Georgetown
University).

One of the most striking examples of this type
of article is to be found in the April 3rd issue of
The Catholic Reporter, weekly newspaper of the
diocese of Kansas City. A very searching article
on conjugal love and responsible parenthood by
Prof. William V. D'Antonio of Notre Dame is
accompanied by an editorial in which the press-
ing need for public discussion of these issues by
Catholics is emphasized, even though such open
discussion may be shocking to those Catholics
"who still regard the teaching Church as an
'answer machine' which produces instantaneous
correct responses to complicated moral questions
without human effort or puzzlement." It is important to note that such statements can be
made by Catholics without being disloyal to the
teaching of their Church. It precisely is an effort
to discover the meaning of that teaching that
such statements are made.

Understanding Catholic Ecclesiology

At another level, a growing understanding of
Catholic ecclesiology will help the Protestant to
realize that when his Catholic friends speak of
the teaching of their Church, they are referring
to the witness of Christian tradition down
through the centuries, to the accumulated and
progressively refined wisdom of all those who are
led by the Spirit of Christ. He will understand
that popes and bishops give authoritative articu-

lation to this tradition, but do not create it: it is
an awareness, a *consensus* that arises in the consciences of the People of God through the guidance of the Holy Spirit, not something that is
imposed on them from without.

He will note that the exact content and significance of this tradition is always open to more
thorough historical and rational investigation. A
book such as *The Theology of Marriage* by
Joseph Kerns, S.J. (Sheed and Ward, 1964), will
be seen as a notable advance in the direction of
an ever fuller understanding of the Christian
tradition on marriage, for it illustrates not only
the continuity and progressive refinement of that
tradition, but also its moments of discordance
and ambiguity.

Another encouraging note will be seen in the
increasingly positive attitude being taken by
Catholics toward the social and behavioral sciences, and toward philosophical syntheses other
than the scholastic. The popularity of authors
such as Marc Oraison *(Love or Constraint)*,
Ignace Lepp *(The Psychology of Loving)*, and
the enthusiasm with which the thought of Ga-
briel Marcel is being received on Catholic cam-
puses will help the Protestant to see that his
Catholic friends are as interested as he is in
exploring the human mystery in all its dimensions and depth.

He will understand, too, that not all teaching
takes place in the classroom or pulpit, and will
see in the works of fiction of such Catholics as
Francois Mauriac, Graham Greene, Georges Ber-
nanos and J. F. Powers—to cite only a few—an
openness to the fuller dimensions of the human

and Christian problem than would seem to be accounted for in the average handbook of theology.

Reformulating Unchanged Values

Finally, the Protestant will observe among Catholic bishops and theologians a new willingness to acknowledge a process of evolution in the development of Christian doctrine, a readiness to distinguish between *values*, which are unchanging, and the manner in which these values are given concrete expression in a particular age and culture.

An outstanding instance of this type of reformulation is currently taking place with respect to the Catholic understanding of religious liberty. When Bishop de Smedt introduced this schema into the Council for deliberation, he pointed out that it is only in the perspective of a process of evolution that we can correctly understand "many pontifical documents which in the 19th century treated of religious liberty in such words that this liberty appeared as something that had to be condemned" *(Council Speeches of Vatican II;* edited by Hans Küng, Yves Congar, and Daniel O'Hanlon; Paulist Press *Deus Books,* 1964, p. 246).

But this type of evolution can also be verified in the realm of marrage ethics. Faith in God's providence and respect for the gift of life are values which at one time were thought to be best expressed in the ideal of the large family; we now know that they can be adequately expressed in the goal of a family consciously limited in its size. As recently as ten years ago theologians considered the use of rhythm to be acceptable only in cases of clearly defined necessity, and then only with the permission of one's confessor; today its application is generally acknowledged to be a normal part of the exercise of responsible parenthood.

Most recently, a few theologians have suggested that the use of the pill can be justified for those who have sufficient reason to employ periodic continence (*cf.* an article in the March issue of *Jubilee* by Rev. Michael O'Leary of Sacred Heart Seminary, Detroit; and an article in the April issue of *Ephermerides Theologicae Lovaniensis* by Fr. Louis Janssens, of the Louvain theological faculty). In more general terms, the need to discover a more liberal approach has been echoed in recent articles by theologians of the stature of H. van der Marck, O.P. and Edward Schillebeeckx (*cf.* an article by the latter in *De Nieuwe Linie*, Dec. 12, 1963).

Among episcopal statements on the subject of family values, that of Bishop Bekkers of Holland (*Herder Correspondence*, Oct. 1963) recommends itself for its constructive openness and for the emphasis which it places upon the personal conscience as the final norm of moral conduct. A statement issued by the Dutch hierarchy prior to the second session of the Council (reported in *Herder Correspondence*, April, 1964) gives evidence of a sympathetic awareness on the part of the bishops of the complexity of the problems confronting married Christians in our times, and a readiness to suspend judgment on these matters until the problem has been explored as thoroughly as possible.

Constructive Ecumenical Dialogue

In the light of these developments, it seems to me that conditions are evolving in which a constructive ecumenical dialogue on the theme of Christian marriage, including the sensitive issue of birth regulation, is becoming a real possibility. Let it be repeated that no one should expect such a dialogue to be easy, or to result in an early solution to our differences. Because of the bitterness that has often surrounded the discussion of these matters in the past, it will be especially necessary that both sides refrain from recrimination, and listen to each other with respect and a real desire to understand, as they bear witness to the meaning which marriage has for them in the light of their faith and experience. But let us not be discouraged by the obstacles either. Convinced of each other's good faith, and conscious of the common experience that is shared by sincere and serious married people everywhere, it must surely be possible that we can reflect together on the meaning of that experience.

Part V

CHRISTIANS
AND JEWS

22

The Ecumenical Movement and the Jews

Gregory Baum

DOES the ecumenical conversation among the Christian Churches also include the Jews as partners? The first answer is, of course, negative. The ecumenical movement strives for the unity of all who believe and are baptized in Christ, and hence it is concerned primarily with Christians. The realities which are discussed in the ecumenical dialogue, the person, office and gifts of Christ, the newness of life which he has brought and the glory which he will reveal at the end of time, are all meaningless to members of the Synagogue who accept the Old Testament, understood in the light of their own rabbinical tradition.

This, however, is not all that can be said in the matter. If ecumenical dialogue stands for the new approach to those outside the Church, implying a careful listening, the sincere attempt to understand the others, the readiness to acknowledge the truth in their criticism of ourselves, and the willingness to change and be conformed more closely to the Gospel, then Christians are able to enter into ecumenical dialogue with Jews.

Jewish-Christian Dialogue

This kind of dialogue has, in fact, taken place for some time, and results have not been wanting. Christians have been led to re-examine their attitude toward the Jews. They have carefully analyzed their teaching and their liturgy to see if these have, in any way, contributed to a movement of hate in the world. The result of these examinations has been devastating. Christians, of all the Churches, have discovered that in popular preaching, in certain liturgical formulas, and often even in serious theological studies we have misrepresented the New Testament doctrine on the Jews. We have drawn a picture of the Jews which aroused contempt and misrepresented their role in the Scriptures.

In order to glorify the New Covenant, we have often been led to belittle the Old and to create an artificial opposition between them, sometimes even contrasting the God of the Old Testament with the God of the New. We have often pretended that God broke the Old Covenant because of Israel's infidelity, and made a new one with the Gentiles; while the orthodox teaching of the Church, expressed in Scripture and liturgy, is that God has fulfilled and confirmed the Old Covenant in the New, making it more spiritual, universal and final.

We have often pretended, moreover, that all

the Jews rejected Jesus. We have ceased to recall in our books and sermons that those who accepted our Lord such as Mary, the apostles, the disciples, and the Church of Jerusalem were also Jews, as was Jesus himself. In the perspective we had chosen, the word "Jew" came to stand for one who denies the Lord.

Finally, we have often created the impression that the Jews were rejected by Jesus, that they were under a divine curse, a people set aside for a perpetual punishment. The New Testament speaks indeed of the chastisement of the responsible leaders of Jerusalem and of the generation contemporary with Jesus—chastisement which was visited upon them in the destruction of Jerusalem—but there is no word in the Scriptures about a perpetual rejection and a punishment to be inflicted on future generations. We read, in fact, the very opposite. According to St. Paul (Romans 11), the unbelieving section of the Jewish people shall nonetheless be protected by God's special providence and, at the moment of the Lord's choosing, return to the kingdom established by Christ.

The ecumenical approach to the Jews is concerned with rectifying these false and harmful expressions of Christian doctrine. This purification has taken place on many levels, yet, it is by no means complete. Notions and attitudes that have been handed down for centuries cannot disappear overnight. The popes themselves have aided in this movement by purifying the liturgy of Good Friday of misleading expressions. In several countries commissions have been set up to examine catechisms and school books in regard to their attitude toward the Jews and the manner of announcing the Christian Gospel, and the new catechisms which have appeared have been corrected and brought into greater conformity with Bible and liturgy.

Pertinent Publications

What are some of the publications in which these questions are discussed and elaborated? We shall confine ourselves to the Catholic side of the movement. (Protestants have worked in the same direction, but their approach has varied, depending on the particular dogmatic commitment.)

One of the Catholic pioneers of the movement is P. Démann, the editor of *Cahier Sioniens*, a periodical dedicated to dialogue with Jews, which began in 1947, but which, unfortunately, has ceased to appear regularly. Equally important is the *Freiburger Rundbrief*, published once a year by G. Luckner and others (Office: Werthmannplatz 4, Freiburg i. Br., Germany). In English there is the widely read yearbook *The Bridge*, edited by J. Oesterreicher (Seton Hall University, Newark, N. J.) of which four volumes have appeared. Another substantial publication in English, giving an up-to-date survey of what is happening in the dialogue between Christians and Jews, is *The Jews and Ourselves*, published twice a year by the Sisters of Our Lady of Sion and distributed from their center in Paris, 61, rue N.D. des Champs, Paris 6e. The only book in English by a Catholic author dealing with the New Testament doctrine on the Jews and the later tendencies to misunderstand it, is G. Baum's *The Jews and the Gospel*, Newman Press, 1961.

Since the result of the Christian-Jewish dialogue must be spread among the people to influence their attitude toward their neighbors, the Sisters of Our Lady of Sion produce two popular bulletins, appearing at regular intervals, destined for wide circulation in schools and homes. *At the Crossroads* is put out by the Ratisbonne Center, 3823 Locust Street, Kansas City 9, Mo. and *Dialogue* (in English and in French) at 4701 Dornal Ave., Montreal 26, Que., Canada.

What has been the effect of the ecumenical dialogue on Jews? We certainly find that Jewish literature has been greatly influenced by Christian thought. The proclamation of Christian doctrine without quarrel and argument has stimulated Jews to find similar or related teachings in the Old Testament and their own traditions.

We notice, moreover, the development of a new attitude toward the person of Jesus. In many Jewish writers, Jesus has come to be regarded as a great Jew, a prophet even, a just man preaching what was best and highest in the tradition of Israel.

Israel And Christian Unity

Quite apart from the dialogue between Christians and Jews there is an inevitable link between the Jewish people and the Christian ecumenical movement. The Jewish people, by the position assigned to them in the Scriptures, are related to the problem of Christian unity in the following three ways:

(1) Trying to understand their divided situation, Christians are driven to examine the schisms recorded in the Bible. We read of the

first schism, pattern of all the subsequent ones, between the kingdom of the north and the kingdom of the south, recorded in 3 Kings; and we hear of the final split in the Jewish people provoked by the person of Jesus. Must not our own Christian understanding of the divisions of Christians take into account God's government of the ancient people of God? "All things happened to them (the people of Israel) as a type and they were written for our correction, upon whom the final age of the world has come" (1 Cor. 10, 11).

(2) The quest for Christian unity and the anguish at our divided state makes us conscious that the Church still lives in the age of expectation. It is true that, compared with the time of the Old Covenant, we belong to the new age of fulfillment; but facing the misery of our divisions, we are deeply aware that we are still on pilgrimage, awaiting the complete fulfillment of the last day. Seen in this perspective, the Church remains in the situation of Israel. In the light of the *parousia*, the Church appears as a community in exile, traveling through the desert, exposed to temptation and sin, unfaithful because of human frailty and faithful because God is faithful. Hence the divine government of, and the divine message addressed to, the ancient Israel are meaningful to the Church now, and this not only because we experience the fulfillment of what is promised, but also because we share in the poverty proper to the exile.

Since the realities of the Old Testament retain a deep meaning for us, dialogue with believing Jews is a fruitful undertaking. We have to ask ourselves all the time whether we have taken the message of the Old Testament seriously enough, whether we have not prematurely neutralized the teachings of Israel, regarding them as replaced by the newness brought by Christ. Have we always announced the good news of creation? Have we always sought a biblical understanding of man's social life and attributed sufficient importance to our existence in this world?

(3) The Christian ecumenical dialogue leads to the Jewish people for yet another reason. We have mentioned above that the return of the Jewish people to Christ's kingdom is an integral part of Christian hope. In this sense, therefore, we may say that the Church is incomplete without Israel. We learn in the New Testament that the holy remnant of Israel became the foundation of the Church. The Church of Jerusalem built upon the Twelve was the stem onto which the Gentile Christians were grafted. However as long as the unbelieving section of Israel remains outside, something is lacking in the Church. We cannot clearly define what is lacking, because St. Paul does not explain his thought at length, but he does announce that the reception of the Jews, in God's own time, will be "life from the dead" (Rom. 11, 15). While we believe that the Catholic Church is the community of the Lord possessing the unity he has given her, we also confess that this unity is perfectible as long as the present age lasts. Christian unity will not be perfect without Israel.

23

What the Vatican Council Could Do for the Jews

Gregory Baum

THE purpose of the Vatican Council is to re-
new Catholic life, and to adapt the Church's
discipline to the needs of the modern day. It is,
therefore, a purely Catholic affair. While representatives from other communions may be present as observers, the Council will not be in
dialogue with them. It is clear, on the other
hand, from the words of Pope John, that the
Council will seek to formulate and direct the renewal of Catholic life with an eye to the problems
of Christian unity and the questions of those
outside the Church. In this sense, the Council is
to be an expression of charity toward all men.

It is, at first sight, by no means obvious what
the Council can do for Christian unity. Only as
we study the problems that separate Christians
more carefully do we discover that the Catholic
Church can do a great deal to remove obstacles

to the unity which all Christians seek. Since the divine structure of the Church is incarnate in a contingent historical situation, it may happen that this human face of the Church does not announce her divine mystery with clarity. The human face of the Church may at times obscure certain areas of Christian revelation. Whenever our Christian life is not in perfect harmony with the Gospel, we, the members of the Church, are setting up obstacles to Christian unity and to the reconciliation of the world with Christ.

It is in this light that the Vatican Council will look upon the reform of the Church. This, at least, is our hope. The renewal of Catholic life is to be the Church's contribution to Christian unity and to the peace of the human family. Yet, since this kind of thinking is rather new in the Catholic Church, the Vatican Council will only begin the process of critically examining the various areas of ecclesiastical life and of suggesting reforms of some of the more obvious shortcomings. The Council will not be the climax, but rather the starting point of the ecumenical movement in the Church.

What can the Council do in regard to the Jewish people? Again, it is by no means obvious what this question could mean. A dialogue between the highest authority in the Church and various representatives of Jewish religion would not lead to anything, not only because it would be difficult to find a truly representative body of Jewish leaders, but for the more profound reason that the Catholic Church is divided from the Synagogue by her faith in Jesus Christ and that, therefore, religious negotiations seem pointless.

Looking at the problem more deeply, however, we discover that there is a great deal the Catholic Church could do in order to remove obstacles separating Christians and Jews and to announce more clearly the love which she has for the people of Israel as for all peoples in the world. From the preceding paragraphs it appears that the ecumenical movement has generated a new kind of humility among Christians. We have begun to ask ourselves to what extent we ourselves are responsible for the lack of faith and the indifference to religion by which we are surrounded. Have we presented an image of the Church which has obscured her charity? Have we insisted on certain doctrines without emphasizing, in proper proportion, the complementary aspects of Catholic teaching? Have we let ourselves be tempted by the spirit of the world and adopted attitudes and opinions derived, not from the Gospel, but from the unredeemed area of the human heart?

By creating this new humility in us, the ecumenical movement has made a tremendous contribution to the Christian understanding of the Jewish problem. We have begun to examine ourselves to determine to what extent we are responsible for the estrangement of the Jews from the Christian Church. And we have found, first, that there are moral principles implied in the Gospel which have not been announced clearly and forcefully enough and, secondly, that we have often let ourselves be influenced by unfounded fables about the Jews contrary to the Church's teaching. Reforming ourselves in these areas is the necessary and important contribution of the

Church to better understanding and greater charity between Christians and Jews. In this way, moreover, we are able to make a more powerful proclamation of the good news to all men.

In the following we shall briefly discuss the two areas where the Second Vatican Council could clarify and assert the Catholic position and thus establish and confirm the brotherhood which should exist between Christians and Jews. That this brotherhood is really the deep intention of the Church was clearly expressed by Pope John XXIII, in a speech to representatives of the United Jewish Appeal in October 1960: "True, there is a great difference between one who accepts only the Old Testament and one who joins the New to it as supreme law and guide. This distinction, however, does not suppress the brotherhood that springs from their common origin, for we are all sons of the same heavenly Father; among us all there must be ever the brightness of love and its practice."

1. General Principles

There is first of all a general principle which is part of biblical revelation: the dignity of the human person as the image of God. In a world which looks upon human beings as pawns or numbers and, worse, which directs its hatred to groups of men as a whole, for biological, ethnic, or religious reasons, it is of paramount importance that the Church openly and solemnly declare that man is created in the image of God and that henceforth his unique dignity and sublime destiny differentiates him from, and lifts

him above, all other creatures of the visible universe. Announcing this biblical vision of man, the
Church would condemn all forms of racism and
organized hatred, and make a positive effort,
significant in our context, to curb any form of
anti-Semitism in the world.

These are the truths the people of our day are
eager to hear. Man hungers after the knowledge
of what he really is, Monsignor Oesterreicher
recently wrote in an article on our topic; and it
is the Church's task to announce the divine revelation of what is man's call and nature.

Over and above the religious respect due to all
men, there is a further moral principle contained
in the biblical vision of human destiny. When we
contemplate the doctrine of the Bible that man
is created in the image of God, that he is appointed to serve and to love his Creator, and that
his destiny is to be united to his eternal Father
in faith and, ultimately, in full possession, we
discover that there is an area of the human personality which is sacred and into which no one,
neither individual nor collectivity, has the right to
enter. Unless the freedom for the spiritual is protected by society, a man might never reach the
happiness for which he is destined. Religious
liberty is a good announced in the Scriptures.
Even the true and final religion revealed by God
himself will not profit a man if it is imposed upon him against his choice. For this reason, the
Church should announce, along with the dignity
of the human person, the ideal of religious liberty
for all men, and insist that governments everywhere respect this good as part of man's natural
endowment. It is obvious to anyone who knows

the problems of the modern world and especially those between religious groups, that the declaration of these two principles by the Vatican Council would be a significant contribution to Christian unity, to a deeper sense of brotherhood with the Jewish people, and to the peace and reconciliation of the whole human family.

2. Specific Doctrines

Apart from the general principles of human dignity and religious liberty, there are more specific points in regard to the Jewish people which the Vatican Council could clarify.

Since the Jews have appeared in our literature as a strange people, a blinded and hard-hearted race, and since moreover they have often been identified by our preachers with the enemies of Jesus, it would be the just and charitable thing to assert in unequivocal language the intimate relationship of the Jewish people to the Christian Church.

Once we begin to reflect on the matter, we see how absurd it is to emphasize that Judas, the Pharisees and the priestly caste opposing Christ were Jews, without mentioning at the same time that Jesus himself was a Jew and that his mother and his disciples were all Jews. In fact the early Church, the community of Jerusalem, was entirely made up of Jews. In the popular imagination the enemies of Jesus are more Jewish than his friends, and the Lord himself has ceased to be the Jew who is "the Light of revelation to the Gentiles and the glory of (his) people Israel." Though the Catholic Church celebrates the circumcision of the Lord on the 1st of January, the

Jewish origin of Jesus has not deeply sunk into the hearts of vast numbers of Christians.

To think of the Jews as those who rejected Jesus is simply untrue. It is against the testimony of the Scriptures. We know from the New Testament that the coming of the Lord divided Israel. The friends of Christ were Jews, and so were his enemies. This in fact is the meaning of Simeon's prophecy: "This child is destined to bring about the fall of many and the rise of many in Israel." While it is true that in the Gospel of St. John the term "the Jews" is usually attached to the enemies of Christ, the group called the priests and Pharisees in the other Gospels, the same fourth Gospel also makes it clear that Jesus identified himself with his people in the phrase "Salvation is from the Jews." Since all the events of our salvation took place within Israel, and since the Gentiles entered the picture only later, after the establishment of the Church, it is obvious that the enemies of Christ as well as the faithful of his day were members of the Jewish people.

For the sake of truth and greater charity, these facts should be recalled to the Christian people.

We must go one step further in removing the feeling of strangeness from the Jews and discover our close connection with them. Israel is related to us not only through the memory of the Church's early days; Israel is alive in the Church of today. We carry Israel in our midst; or more correctly, to follow the idiom of St. Paul, Israel carries us as the stem carries the branches. The ancient covenant which God announced to Abraham and established through Moses has been fulfilled by Jesus, fulfilled, renewed, universalized, made eternal and spiritual. The community created by the new covenant of Jesus is the true Israel, the continuation of the old, based on the promises made to the patriarchs and the prophets, fulfilled in Jerusalem, embracing the holy remnant of the chosen people. This holy remnant, cleansed by the blood of Christ and renewed in the Spirit, is the Messianic community in which all of the nations of the world shall find their salvation. This community, the Catholic Church, is founded and built up on the Israel of God's choice.

Israel in our midst is not a vague memory of the past. We venerate the Scriptures of the Old Covenant as the Word of God addressed to us now. The same Holy Spirit speaks to us in the Old and New Testaments which, together, constitute our Bible. We venerate the saints of the Old Covenant in our liturgy, Abraham is our patriarch, and the fathers and prophets of Israel are our brethren interceding before God for the entire Church. The feasts of the Christian Church are the fulfillment of the ancient feasts of Israel. Everytime Christ comes to us in the eucharist he fulfills the ancient passover in his Church. All our sacraments are the fulfillment of the wonderful deeds of God revealed to Israel in the desert, and the coming true of the promises made to us through the voice of the ancient prophets.

Studying the Word of God and the liturgical life of the Church, we discover that Israel is alive in our midst now. If this fact were underlined in proper proportion, Christians would become more conscious of the nearness of the Jewish people to the Church of Christ.

There is a second point concerning the relation of Israel to the Church which deserves to be spelled out in clear terms since it would remove certain widely spread and highly insulting misunderstanding regarding the Jewish people.

Serves Them Right?

There are unfortunately many Christian sermons of the past which claim that the Jews have been rejected by God, that because of their unbelief, or because of the crucifixion, they are now a people under a divine curse, the object of God's grave displeasure and set apart for perpetual punishment in history. Such notions have entered quite deeply into the Christian imagination. The plight and the persecutions of the Jews appeared to some Christians as "proof" of the Gospel of Jesus! In their minds this is God's way of showing that Christ has conquered. And even when they regret the injustices inflicted on innocent people, they might feel that according to divine providence it serves them right.

There is, however, no such doctrine contained in the Scriptures. It is true that the Lord prophesied the chastisement of the unfaithful generation of Jerusalem. He foretold the destruction of Jerusalem, and we know from history that the fall of the holy city took place in the year 70. But there is no reason whatever to extend this punishment announced by Christ to all Jews of that generation nor to the Jews of all generations. It is absurd and wicked to call the Jews a deicide nation! It is absurd and wicked to attribute the guilt for the crucifixion to all Jews of the generation of Jesus or even to the Jews of later centuries. There is indeed a symbolical meaning in the destruction of Jerusalem, but this is not at all a permanent punishment hovering over the Jewish people; it is rather the final judgment on all the nations, to be pronounced on the Last Day, the eschatological background of Christ's teaching. If the destruction of Jerusalem is to make men tremble, then these men are not the Jews but all men, all people, including ourselves.

The Scriptures however are not altogether silent about the destiny of Israel. When it became apparent that the body of the Jewish people were to remain outside the Church, St. Paul announced in his epistle to the Romans, chapter 11, that the eternal God who had once chosen the people of Israel would not, despite their unbelief, abandon them. Israel shall be accompanied by a special divine providence. It shall not lose itself in the world and become altogether like the other nations, for God "whose gifts and promises are without repentance" will recall the people, at the moment of his choice, to enter into the kingdom of their Savior. "I will not have you ignorant of this mystery," St. Paul tells the Roman Christians, "or else you might have too good a conceit of yourselves. Blindness has fallen on a part of Israel, but only until the tale of the Gentile nations is complete: then the whole of Israel shall find salvation." Thanks to the everlasting fidelity of God and not due to anything in themselves, the Jewish people remain the bearers of a special promise the fulfillment of which is still in the future. Our Christian vision of history is not complete, and our hope in Christ's victory not integral, unless we become more conscious that the Jewish people are inescapably linked to the Christian Church, accompanying it from a distance, destined to be reconciled to it before the end of time.

If this hope were clearly spelled out and announced to the Christian people, our relationship to the Jews would be more deeply formed by the Gospel of universal salvation.

24

The Protestant Christian and the Jews

A. Roy Eckhardt

TODAY the unity of Catholic and Protestant attitudes toward the Jews is remarkable. I am convinced that the majority of contemporary Protestant theologians will be in basic agreement with Father Baum's exposition in "The Ecumenical Movement and the Jews" pages 219-225. I regard the present article as supplement and commentary.

Many Protestant writings on this subject have appeared in just the last few years, while a number of groups are giving fresh attention to it. Perhaps it is not strange that much of the effort is German. The more important studies since 1960 include D. Goldschmidt and H. J. Kraus, eds., *Der Ungekündigte Bund* (Stuttgart: Kreuz-Verlag, 1962), prepared by the Commssion on Jewish-Christian Relations of the German Evangelical *Kirchentag* and based on the latter's 1961 meeting in Berlin; *Israel und die Kirche* (Zurich: EVZ-Verlag, 1961, original in Dutch), produced by the Reformed Council on the Relation between the Church and Israel under commission by the General Synod of the Reformed Church of the Netherlands; J. Jocz, *The Spiritual History of Israel* (London: Eyre and Spottiswoode, 1961); K. Kupisch, *Das Volk der Geschichte, Randbemerkugen zur Geschichte der Judenfrage* (Berlin: Lettner-Verlag, 2d rev. ed., 1960); R. Mayer, *Zum Gespräch mit Israel, Eine theologische Auseinandersetzung* (Stuttgart: Calwer Verlag, 1962); J. Parkes, *The Foundations of Judaism and Christianity* (London: Vallentine, Mitchell & Co., 1960); W. D. Marsch and K. Thieme, eds., *Christen und Juden, Ihr Gegenüber vom Apostelkonzil bis heute* (Göttingen: Vandenoeck & Ruprecht, 1961); and H. T. Schultz, ed., *Juden-Christen-Deutsche* (Stuttgart; Kreuz-Verlag, 1961). (The Marsch-Thieme and Schultz volumes include non-Protestant writers.) There is also an important quarterly *Judaica*, a Protestant publication from Zurich, devoted to the understanding of Jews and Judaism.

In Germany some thirty-six groups and organizations are now concerned with Jewish-Christian cooperation and with the encounter between Christians and Jews; Protestants are participating in many of these. Since the integration in 1961 of the International Missionary Council and the World Council of Churches, erstwhile I.M.C., work in this area has been assumed by the Committee on the Church and the Jewish People, a constituent part of the Division of World Mission and Evangelism of the W.C.C. In the United States, the Central Department of Evangelism of the National Council of the Churches of Christ includes a Committee on the Christian Approach to the Jews. At denominational, established and confessional levels a number of Church bodies in the United States, Canada, Great Britain and Europe maintain corresponding divisions or societies.

II

I think that the recent Protestant situation can be summed up as follows: (1) In the literature and in Church pronouncements a considerable trend has appeared away from an execrative and judgmental stance vis-à-vis the Jews and Jewish faith. (2) A once-prevalent liberal latitudinarianism, still dominant among Americans, has been countered by a stress on the uniqueness and even the finality of Christian faith, although with an attempt to avoid the idea of *die Absolutheit des Christentums*. (Whether this latter distinction can be vindicated practically is, of course, problematic.) (3) The consequence of points one and two taken together is a certain measure of uncertainty. Pious absolutists could damn the Jews, while liberal relativists could bless everybody; those two sides, though entirely opposed, could share the peace of having a neat solution. But what if God's choice of Israel entails an everlasting bond, and yet the Christ has appeared! Tension in substance and perplexity in thought are made inevitable.

Theologically stated, we are brought hard against the fact of the divine mystery—with respect not only to the Jews but to the double mystery of Israel and the Church. George S. Hendry reminds us that for St. Paul the pre-eminent mystery is the inclusion of the Gentiles in the divine purpose of salvation (*A Theological Word Book of the Bible*, ed. A. Richardson, New York: Macmillan, 1952, p. 156). This means that when I as a Gentile encounter the Jews, the really vital question I face is not, how are *they* to be saved? but rather, how am I to be brought into the unbreakable covenant with Israel? For St. Paul and for the entire Christian Church the answer is that only a Jew can accomplish such an unspeakable work. This Jew is Jesus of Nazareth who is also—some may add "and therefore" — the only-begotten Son of the Father. "God's choice stands"; the Jews "are his friends for the sake of the patriarchs ... How unsearchable his judgments, how untraceable his ways!" (Rom. 11, 28, 33). Christ is the Second Adam; may we not also think of him as the Second Abraham, who as the Jew of Nazareth and the Son of God can be truly Patriarch to all men, including those outside the covenant? Jesus makes universally historical the theological judgment, "It is from the Jews that salvation comes" (John 4, 22).

The observant will immediately respond that the foregoing sentiment does not take into account the ever-present Christian of Jewish origin; however, I am speaking in existential terms. There is a more objective way of putting the matter: Recognition of *Heilsgeschichte* opens the way to a distinctive and positive attitude toward the Jews and Judaism. Between Jewish faith and Christian faith basic differences obtain; to elab-

orate on them is not necessary here. I may simply note that I believe J. Coert Rylaersdam has
a point in maintaining, as I heard him do in
conversation, that the eschatological difference
between Jews and Christians today is more profound than the christological difference, *i.e.*, the
Jew rejects the Christian announcement of fulfillment, the triumph over sin and death. But
the unity of the two faiths is just as fundamental.
"Brotherhood," that well-meaning but traditionally extra-theocentric notion, is counteracted and
yet fulfilled by the persuasion that the Jew is
older brother and the Christian is younger brother
within the joyous household of salvation.

III

As evidenced in its ecumenical deliberations
and pronouncements and in its theological discussions, Protestantism discloses its uncertainty
through the issue of "the Christian mission to
the Jews." Is not the Christian Church obligated
to proclaim the Gospel to the children of Israel
as well as to the other men? Is there not an implicit anti-Semitism in any refusal to do so? The
traditional answer to these questions has of
course been "yes." I may report that a rather different emphasis appears in some recent Protestant thinking, but not in a way which implies
that "one faith is as good as another."

The position to which I refer comprises an in-
dependently Christian counterpart of the views
of such Jewish thinkers as Franz Rosenzweig
and Will Herberg, for whom Israel looks inward
to the Jews while Christianity looks outward to

the Gentiles, bringing them to the God of Israel (Herberg, *Judaism and Modern Man*, New York: Farrar, Straus and Young, 1951, p. 272). Paul Tillich understands the unique function of Judaism in terms of the perennial conflict between the pagan, polytheistic "gods of space" and the living "Lord of time," and applies this function to the place of the Jews in a "Christian" culture: It is Judaism's function "to guard the spirit of the prophets—against itself, against national groups, and against the Churches, whenever they fall prey to the demands of space. The Jews are and must remain the people of time" (*Die Judenfrage, ein christliches und ein deutsches Problem*, Berlin: Gebruder Weiss Verlag, 1953, p. 37). And Karl Barth conceives the permanence of the Jewish people in history as a sign of the faithfulness of God: "They could and can disappear just as little as God's faithfulness can come to an end" (*Against the Stream*, New York: Philosophical Library, 1954, pp. 196-7).

I may perhaps be permitted to record a few tentative thoughts of my own. Any point of view which at once defends the right of human conscience and takes the history of faith with genuine seriousness will find a certain necessity in the denial of the divinity of Christ among Jews who have been exposed to the Christian message across the years. This is not alone because of the strong association of that message with persecutions of the Jews, but also because it is blasphemous for the believing Jew to attest that any man is God. And how could the Christian conscience ever summon people to such a sin as blasphemy? But it must be noted that this moral reservation need not mean the sale of one's soul to "liberalism" or "relativism." After all, it is orthodox Christianity to state that *any* man's acknowledgment of the lordship of Christ must involve a miracle; "no one can say 'Jesus is Lord!' except under the influence of the Holy Spirit" (1 Cor. 12, 3). We need not question the legitimacy of the Christian witness to Israel, but such witness must not spend itself in assaulting spiritual ramparts from which Jews cannot in all conscience descend. The Christian ethic of solidarity with all men forbids this. We must meet the Jews upon the heights.

Is there a Christian parallel to the contention in some Jewish theology that the role of the Church is to make all men Jews, *i.e.*, to bring the Gentile into the covenant with the Holy One of Israel? Can we speak in a positively Christian manner about the place of the Jews in the divine economy of salvation—in ways that will (a) be distinctive as against the somewhat effete expression of a "conversionist" stance vis-à-vis Jews; (b) mediate (aufheben) a dialogic relation between Judaism and Christianity; and (c) maintain the historical uniqueness of Christian faith? I submit that from the Christian side the peculiar covenantal relation between the Jews and God is seen to remain in force through the very historical fact of Jesus the Jew — the "great brother" of whom, indeed, Martin Buber speaks. To behold Jesus as the only-begotten Man but, more, as the special historical prototype of what the Jew can be and can become—adorer of the one true God and lover of human-kind—is to have a vantage ground for confronting many issues within the Jewish-Christian *Auseinander-setzung*. Whatever the decisions of individual Jews, we must witness that it is Israel's calling to remain faithful to its promises to Yahweh through (as the Christian would have it) Jesus the Jew, or (as the Jew would say) through that steadfastness in the presence of the Holy One which purges away all idolatries and commits itself to sublime justice.

IV

Hard study and prayerful attention to the mystery of Israel by Catholics and Protestants together will not only strengthen the ties between the Church and Israel but fasten the ecumenical bond of Christians. Strangely, redemption has a way of drawing near as men look away from themselves. "How unsearchable his judgments, how untraceable his ways!"

25

A Short Bibliography of Ecumenical Literature

Paul Broadhurst

This is a select bibliography, by no means exhaustive, of works bearing on the ecumenical movement which have been written in or translated into English. Except in the section "Periodicals," no mention has been made of the many French and German publications. Where it has been thought helpful, a short descriptive note is provided.

A. Works by Catholic Authors

ADAM, KARL. *One and Holy.* New York: Sheed and Ward, 1951, 130p. An approach to Lutheran-Catholic accord in Germany.

ALGERMISSEN, KONRAD. *Christian Denominations.* St. Louis: B. Herder, 1945. 1051p. A descriptive survey of Christian communities, Catholic, Protestant and Orthodox.

ATTWATER, DONALD. *The Christian Churches of the East.* Milwaukee: Bruce, 1961 (revised). Vol. 1: Churches in communion with Rome. 248p. Vol. 2: Churches not in communion with Rome. (1962) 272p.

Baum, Gregory, O.S.A. *That They May Be One*. Westminster: Newman, 1958. 181p. A study of papal doctrine, Leo XIII to Pius XII.

— *Progress and Perspectives*. New York: Sheed and Ward, 1962, 251p. The Catholic quest for Christian unity.

Bea, Augustin Cardinal, S.J. *The Unity of Christians*. New York: Herder and Herder, 1963. 231p. Writings, addresses and interviews of Cardinal Bea.

Bouyer, Louis, C.Or. *The Spirit and Forms of Protestantism*. Westminster: Newman, 1956. 234 p.

— *The Word, the Church and Sacraments in Protestantism and Catholicism*. New York: Desclee, 1961. 80 p.

Boyer, Charles, S.J. *Christian Unity*. New York: Hawthorn, 1962. 131 p.

Cary-Elwes, Columba. *The Sheepfold and the Shepherd*. London: Longmans, Green, 1961. 335 p. The principles of Catholic ecumenism.

Congar, Yves, O.P. *After Nine Hundred Years*. New York: Fordham University Press, 1959. 160 p. The background of the schism between the Eastern and Western Churches.

— *Divided Christendom*. London, Geoffrey Bles, 1939. 298 p. The first technical survey of the ecumenical problem from the viewpoint of Catholic theology.

Duff, Edward. *The Social Thought of the World Council of Churches*. New York: Association Press, 1956. 339 p.

Dumont, Christophe, O.P. *Approaches to Christian Unity*. Baltimore: Helicon, 1959. 226 p. Christian unity from a liturgical and spiritual standpoint.

ENGLERT, CLEMENT, C.Ss.R. *Catholics and Orthodox: Can They Unite?* New York: Paulist Press, 1961. 127 p.

HARDON, JOHN, S.J. *Christianity in Conflict.* Westminster: Newman, 1959. 300 p. An evaluation of Protestant belief and practice.

HEENAN, JOHN (ed.) *Christian Unity: A Catholic View.* London: Sheed and Ward, 1962. 198 p. An account of the first official conference organized by the English Bishops' Committee for Christian Unity.

HEMMER, HYPPOLYTE. *Fernand Portal, 1855-1926, Apostle of Unity.* New York: St. Martins Press, 1961. 181 p. A participant in the Malines Conversations between Catholics and Anglicans (1921-1926) writes about one of his collaborators.

JAEGER, LORENZ. *The Ecumenical Council, the Church and Christendom.* London: Chapman, 1961. 211 p.

KUNG, HANS. *The Council, Reform and Reunion.* New York: Sheed and Ward, 1961. 219 p.

LEEMING, BERNARD, S.J. *The Churches and the Church.* Westminster: Newman, 1960. 340 p. The Catholic Church's participation in the ecumenical movement.

LORTZ, JOSEPH. *How the Reformation Came About.* New York: Herder and Herder, 1964. 115 p. A popular survey by a noted German historian of his classic work, *Reformation in Germany.*

MCNALLY, ROBERT. *Reform of the Church.* New York: Herder and Herder, 1963. 140 p. An insight into the Church and reform through an examination of the late middle ages.

McNamara, Kevin. (ed.) *Christian Unity*. Maynooth, 1962.

Maximos IV Sayegh. (ed.) *The Eastern Churches and Catholic Unity*. New York: Herder and Herder, 1963. 236 p. Some of the most distinguished prelates of the Eastern Catholic Churches reflect on the importance of Catholic openness to every culture and form of organzation compatible with the unity of faith and charity.

North American Liturgical Week. *The Liturgy and Unity in Christ*. *Washington*: The Liturgical Conference, 1961. 138 p.

Pol, William van de. *The Christian Dilemma*. New York: Philosophical Library, 1952. 317 p.

Problems Before Unity. Baltimore: Helicon, 1962. 158 p. Papers given by Catholic theologians from North America and Europe at a 1961 Graymoor conference.

St. John, Henry, O.P. *Essays in Christian Unity 1928-1954.* . *Westminster*: *Newman*, 1955. 164 p. Essays written over a 25-year period, manifesting development of thought in the field of Christian unity.

Sartory, Thomas, O.S.B. *The Oecumenical Movement and the Unity of the Church*. Oxford: Blackwell, 1963. 310 p. An historical and systematic treatment.

Sherwood, Polycarp, O.S.B. (ed.) *The Unity of the Church of God*. Baltimore: Helicon, 1963. Essays on the Eastern Churches in communion with Rome.

Stephenson, Lillian. *Max Josef Metzger, Priest and Martyr*. New York: Macmillan, 1952. 149 p. Portrait of the founder of the German Una Sancta brotherhood.

SWIDLER, LEONARD. (ed.) *Dialogue for Reunion.* New York: Herder and Herder, 1962. 88 p. Bishop Wright, Reinhold and Tavard write on the ecumenical movement, on the liturgy and on tradition.

TAVARD, GEORGES, A.A. *The Catholic Approach to Protestantism.* New York: Harper, 1955. 160 p.

— *Protestant Hopes and Catholic Responsibility.* Notre Dame: Fides, 1960. 63 p. A short introduction to the basic principles of Catholic ecumenism.

— *Protestantism.* New York: Hawthorn, 1959. 139 p.

— *Two Centuries of Ecumenism.* Notre Dame: Fides, 1960. 250 p. An historical survey of ecumenism in the 19th and 20th centuries.

TAYLOR, M. J., S.J. *The Protestant Liturgical Renewal.* Westminster: Newman, 1963. 357 p.

TODD, JOHN. *Catholicism and the Ecumenical Movement.* London: Longmans, Green, 1956. 111 p. The significance for Catholics of the World Council of Churches and the movement which it represents.

VILLAIN, MAURICE. *Unity.* Baltimore: Helicon, 1963. 381 p. A brief history of the ecumenical movement and reflections on Catholic ecumenism.

WEIGEL, GUSTAVE, S.J. *A Catholic Primer on the Ecumenical Movement.* Westminster: Newman, 1958. 79 p.

— *Catholic Theology in Dialogue.* New York: Harper, 1961. 126 p. Lectures given by Fr. Weigel to non-Catholic audiences on theological themes of interest to those in search of Christian unity.

— *Churches in North America*. Baltmore: Helicon, 1961. 152 p.

— *Faith and Understanding in America*. New York: Macmillan, 1959. 170 p.

— *A Survey of Protestant Theology in Our Day*. Westminster: Newman, 1954. 58 p. A brief description of contemporary Protestant theology in America.

B. A Few Works by Orthodox, Anglican and Protestant Authors

ASMUSSEN, HANS ET AL. *The Unfinished Reformation*. Notre Dame: Fides, 1961. 213 p. A call by five Lutheran theologians of the Sammlung movement for a catholic reformation in the Evangelical Church and a renewal of the Catholic Church in the spirit of the evangelical tradition.

BELL, G. K. A (ed).) *Documents on Christian Unity*. London: Oxford University Press.
1st and 2nd series: 1920-1930 (selection 1958).
3rd series: 1930-1948 (1948).
4th series: 1948-1957 (1958).

— *The Kingship of Christ*. Baltimore: Penguin, 1954. 183 p. The story of the World Council of Churches.

BENOIT, J. D. *Liturgcal Renewal*. London: SCM Press, 1958. 112 p. Studies in Catholic and Protestant developments in Europe.

BENZ, ERNST. *The Eastern Orthodox Church*. New York: Doubleday, 1963. 236 p. A Lutheran expert on the Eastern Churches writes about the thought and life of Orthodoxy.

BRANDRETH, H. R. *Unity and Reunion: A Bibliography*. London: Adam and Charles Black, 1954 (2nd edition).

BROWN, ROBERT MCAFEE. *The Spirit of Protestantism*. New York: Oxford University Press, 1961. 284 p. One of America's leading Protestant theologians on the origins, history and meaning of Protestantism.

CAVERT, SAMUEL MCCREA. *On the Road to Christian Unity*. New York: Harper, 1961. 192 p. An appraisal of the ecumenical movement by one of the chief architects of the World Council of Churches.

CULLMANN, OSCAR. *Message to Catholics and Protestants*. Grand Rapids: Wm. B. Eerdmans, 1959. 57 p. One of the world's best known Protestant theologians makes a proposal for realizing Christian solidarity in charity.

DILLENBERGER, JOHN AND WELCH, CLAUDE. *Protestant Christianity*. New York: Scribners, 1958. 352 p. An essay on the interpretation of Protestant Christianity in the light of its historical development.

DVORNIK, FRANTISEK. *The Photian Schism; history and legend*. London: Cambridge University Press, 1948. A study of Photius and the schism between Roman and Greek Churches.

GOODALL, NORMAN. *The Ecumenical Movement*. New York: Oxford University Press, 1961.

MACY, PAUL. *If It Be of God*. St. Louis: Bethany Press, 1960. 191 p. The story of the World Council of Churches.

MASCALL, E. L. *The Recovery of Unity*. London: Longmans, Green, 1958. 242 p. An Anglican theologian describes the bedrock realities of disunity and the starting point for any profitable and constructive thinking about reunion.

MEYENDORFF, J. *The Orthodox Church*. New York: Pantheon, 1962. 256 p. An Orthodox priest-theologian writes on his Church — its past and its role today.

MINEAR, PAUL (ed.) *The Nature of the Unity We Seek*. St. Louis: Bethany Press, 1958. 304 p. The official report of the North American Conference on Faith and Order, 1957.

NEILL, STEPHEN. *Towards Church Union*. London: SCM Press, 1952.

NELSON, J. R. (ed.) *Christian Unity in North America*. St. Louis: Bethany Press, 1958. 208 p. The views of eighteen leading Protestant thinkers.

PAWLEY, BERNARD. *Looking at the Vatican Council*. London: SCM Press, 1962. 136 p. The impressions of an official Anglican observer at Vatican II .

PELIKAN, JAROSLAV. *The Riddle of Roman Catholicism*. New York: Abingdon, 1959. 272 p. A Lutheran theologian interprets Catholicism —its history, beliefs and future.

ROUSE, RUTH AND NEILL, STEPHEN (ed.) *A History of the Ecumenical Movement 1517-1948*. Philadelphia: Westminster, 1954. 822 p. A basic reference work.

SCHMEMANN, ALEXANDER. *The Historical Road of Eastern Orthodoxy*. New York: Holt, Rinehart and Winston, 1963. 349 p. A history of Eastern Orthodoxy by a distinguished Orthodox theologian.

SCHUTZ, ROGER. *Unity: Man's Tomorrow.* New York: Herder and Herder, 1962, 94 p. The Prior of Taize views the Christian movement towards unity as an essential means to the effectiveness of Christianity in the world of tomorrow.

SENAUD, A. *Christian Unity: A Bibliography.* Geneva: World's Committee of YMCAs, 1937. 2000 titles (including French and German) from the mid-19th century to 1937.

SKYDSGAARD, KRISTEN. *One in Christ.* Philadelphia: Muhlenberg, 1957. 230 p. An eminent Danish Lutheran theologian explains Protestant and Catholic beliefs, pointing out important similarities and basic differences.

SKYDSGAARD, KRISTEN (ed.) *The Papal Council and the Gospel.* Minneapolis: Augsburg, 1961. 220 p. Seven Protestant theologians present an anticipatory study of various aspects of Vatican II and its importance for Protestants.

THURIAN, MAX. *Visible Unity and Tradition.* Baltimore: Helicon, 1962. 136 p. One of the founders of Taize writes on the visible unity already existing among Christians and provides an appraisal of the common elements among the Churches upon which greater unity can be achieved.

VISSER 'T HOOFT, WILHELM. *Pressure of our Common Calling.* London: SCM Press, 1959. This book, together with the next, is valuable for an understanding of the theology of the World Council of Churches.

—— *The Renewal of the Church.* London: SCM Press, 1956.

VISSER 'T HOOFT, WILHELM (ed.) *The First Assembly of the World Council of Churches. Official Report.* (Amsterdam, 1948). New York: Harper, 1949. 271 p.

—— *The Evanston Report: the Second Assembly of the World Council of Churches.* (Evanston, 1954). New York: Harper, 1955. 368 p.

— *The New Delhi Report: the Third Assembly of the World Council of Churches.* (New Delhi, 1961). New York: Association Press, 1962. 456 p.

The World Council of Churches: Its Process of Formation. Geneva: World Council Publications, 1946. 205 p.

C. Inter-Church Symposia

ASMUSSEN, HANS AND SARTORY, THOMAS, O.S.B. *Lutheran-Catholic: Unity?* Baltimore: Helicon, 1960. A systematic ecumenical conversation between a Lutheran and a Catholic theologian.

BEVAN, R. J. (ed.) *The Churches and Christian Unity.* London: Oxford University Press, 1963. 275 p. A collection of essays—Catholic, Orthodox, Anglican and Protestant—on the principles and problems of ecumenism.

BOSC, J., GUITTON, J., DANIELOU, J. *The Catholic Protestant Dialogue.* Baltimore: Helicon, 1960. 147 p. Two Catholic and one Protestant theologians cooperate in writing on points of convergence and difference among the Churches.

BROWN, ROBERT MCAFEE and WEIGEL, GUSTAVE, S.J. *An American Dialogue.* New York: Doubleday, 1960. 216 p. A Protestant looks at

Catholicism and a Catholic looks at Protestantism.

CALLAHAN, DANIEL (ed.) *Christianity Divided.* New York: Sheed and Ward, 1961. 335 p. Essays by well-known Catholic and Protestant theologians on basic theological issues which divide their Churches.

Christians in Conversation. Westminster: Newman, 1962. 112 p. Papers read at a colloquy of Catholic and Protestant theologians at St. John's Abbey, Collegeville, 1960.

COWAN, WAYNE (ed.) *Facing Protestant-Roman Catholic Tensions.* New York: Association Press, 1960. 125 p. Six Catholic and seven Protestant writers join in dialogue on paper about the principal questions now engaging their Churches.

CRISTIANI, L. AND RILLIET, J. *Catholics and Protestants: Separated Brothers.* Westminster: Newman, 1960. 176 p. An exchange of letters between two distinguished spokesmen.

MORRIS, WILLIAM (ed.) *The Unity We Seek.* Toronto: Ryerson Press, 1962. 160 p. Theologians—Protestant, Orthodox and Catholic —write on the Church and the Churches.

SCHARPER, PHILIP (ed.) *American Catholics: a Protestant-Jewish View.* New York: Sheed & Ward, 1959, 235 p.

Unionistic Congress, 1st. *Proceedings, 1955.* St. Procopius Abbey, 1956. 100 p. Papers given at a meeting of Orthodox and Catholic theologians.

Unionistic Congress, 2nd and 3rd. *Proceedings, 1957 and 1959.* Benedictine Abbey Press, 1960. 228 p.

D. Periodicals

Eastern Churches Quarterly. (Benedictine Fathers, London). 480 Lexington Ave., New York 17, N.Y.

Ecumenical Press Service. Weekly information bulletin. World Council of Churches, 17, Route de Malagnou, Geneva.

Ecumenical Review. Quarterly. (World Council of Churches). 475 Riverside Drive, New York 25, N.Y.

The Ecumenist. Bi-monthly. 401 W. 59th St., New York 19, N.Y. Published by the Paulist Press in collaboration with the Centre for Ecumenical Studies, St. Michael's College, University of Toronto.

Faith and Order Trends. Quarterly. Department of Faith and Order Studies, National Council of Churches of Christ, 475 Riverside Drive, New York 25, N.Y.

Irenikon. Quarterly. Published in French by the Benedictines of Chevetogne, Belgium.

Istina. Quarterly. Published in French by the Centre d'Etudes 'Istina', 25, Bd. d'Auteuil, Boulogne-sur-Seine, France.

Journal of Ecumenical Studies. Catholic, Protestant, Orthodox. 3 times yearly. Duquesne University Press, Pittsburgh, Pa.

Unitas. Quarterly (Unitas Association, Rome). Graymoor Press, Peekskill, New York.

Verbum Caro. Quarterly. Published in French by Communaute de Taize, Saoneet-Loire, France.

Vers L' Unite Chretienne. Monthly. Published in French by the Centre d'Etudes 'Istina', 25, Bd. d'Auteuil, Boulogne-sur-Seine, France.